Success Principles

CHANGE MY LIFE

Learn What All Successful People Must Go Through To Get To The Mountain Top

Hubert Norris

Table of Contents

Chapter 1: Do You Know What You Want?..6
Chapter 2: *Don't Be Demotivated By Fear*...9
Chapter 3: There's No Time for Regrets 12
Chapter 4: 10 Habits to Change Your Life 16
Chapter 5: 6 Triggers That Make New Habits Stick 23
Chapter 6: 10 Habits to Start Right Now..27
Chapter 7: *5 Habits of Bill Gates*..33
Chapter 8: *The Goal Is Not The Point*...38
Chapter 9: 10 Habits of Jeff Bezos 41
Chapter 10: 5 Habits For An Extremely Productive Day 45
Chapter 11: 10 Habits of Bernard Arnault...49
Chapter 12: 10 Habits of Successful Traders 53
Chapter 13: Ten habits of David Beckham 58
Chapter 14: 6 Habits of Ridiculously Likeable People...................................63
Chapter 15: 10 Habits of Kobe Bryant 68
Chapter 16: 10 Habits of Jack Ma 72
Chapter 17: How To Stop Feeling Overwhelmed..76
Chapter 18: 10 Habits of Warren Buffett 78
Chapter 19: 10 Habits of Cristiano Ronaldo 82
Chapter 20: *Motivation With Good Feelings*..87
Chapter 21: 10 Habits of Steve Jobs..90
Chapter 22: How To Set Smart Goals 94
Chapter 23: 10 Habits of Drake 97
Chapter 24: *Avoid The Dreaded Burnout* 100
Chapter 25: 9 Habits of Highly Successful People...................................... 103
Chapter 26: 10 Habits of Unsuccessful People.. 109
Chapter 27: *Be Motivated by Challenge*... 115
Chapter 28: *Five Habits of Permanent Weight Loss*.................................... 118

Chapter 29: The Magic of Journaling 122
Chapter 30: The 5 Second Rule 125

Chapter 1:
Do You Know What You Want?

Do you know who you are? Do you know what you are? Do you know what you want to become? Do you have any idea what you might become?

Every sane human has asked these questions to themselves multiple times in their lives. We have a specific trait of always finding the right answers to everything. We humans always try to find the meaning behind everything.

It's in our built-in nature to question everything around us. Yet we are here in this modern era of technology and resources and we don't have a sense of purpose. We don't have a true set of goals. We don't give enough importance to our future to take a second and make a long-term plan for longer gains.

The fault in our thinking is that we don't have a strict model of attention. We have too many distractions in our lives to spare a moment to clear our minds.

The other thing that makes us confused or ignorant is the fact that people have a way of leading us into thinking things that are not ours to start with.

Society has made these norms that have absolutely nothing to do with anyone except that these were someone's experience when they were once at our stage. We are dictated on things that are not ours to achieve but only a mere image of what others want us to achieve or don't.

No one has the right to tell you anything. No one has a right to say anything to you except if they are advising or reminding you of the worst. But to inflict a scenario with such surety that it will eventually happen to you because you have a fault that many others had before you is the most superstitious and illogical thing to do on any planet let alone Earth.
No one knows what the future holds for anyone. No one can guarantee even the next breath that they take. So why put yourself under someone else's spell of disappointment? Why do you feel the need to satisfy every person's whim? Why do you feel content with everyone around you getting their ways?

You always know in your heart, deep down in some corner what you want. You will always know what you need to be fulfilled. You will always find an inspiration within yourself to go and pursue that thing. What you need are some self-confidence and some self-motivation. You need to give yourself some time to straighten up your thoughts and you will eventually get the BOLD statement stating 'This is what I want'.

You don't need to shut everyone around you. You just need to fix your priorities and you will get a vivid image of what things are and what they can become.

There is no constraint of age or gender to achieving anything. These are just mental and emotional hurdles that we have imposed on our whole race throughout our history.

Just remember. When you know what you want, and you want it bad enough to give away everything for that, you will someday find a way to finally get it.

Chapter 2:

Don't Be Demotivated By Fear

What are you doing right now? What ambitions do you have for the morning to come? What doubts you have in mind? What is stopping you right now?

You have doubts about anything because you want to be cautious. You are hesitant because you have your gut telling you to think again. The reality is you are afraid and you don't know it. Or maybe you do know it but you keep ignoring your weakness.

That weakness you keep ignoring is your fear. Fear starts with a seed but if left alone can manifest deeper roots and can have a devastating impact on one's personality.

Fear is the biggest enemy of commitment. Fear kills productivity. Fear eats creativity. Fear crushes motivation.

People keep fears as if they are being smart about unexpected outcomes. You don't need to stay afraid of things to abstain from them. The only thing you need to fear is the 'Fear' itself.

When you were a child, your parents motivated you and gave you the confidence to get over most of your fears. But now you would be considered stupid and childish if you seek a mentor. You what do you do?

The answer is simple. You have yourself to try out things that make you take a step back. Because fear is self-imposed. You made yourself prone to such feelings and you can make them go away as well.

Fear can make you second guess your own abilities.

We are way behind our goals because subconsciously we have thought of the failure that can happen. The fear of our dreams shattering overtakes the ambition and happiness when you finally get to the scale. This overburdening feeling of fear keeps us sitting in our seats and stops us from trying out new things. This fear makes us believe that we don't deserve what we have dreamt of.

So I have a question for you! What have you done in the last week, or month or even a year to overcome only the smallest phobia?

If you haven't, it is possible that you won't leave what you have right now and never go for anything more than you can own. This reason is that fear makes you remain content with whatever nature and God have bestowed upon you on time after time. But you won't get up and try to work new things for bigger and better blessings that hard work and some gutsy calls have to offer.

If you can't give up the feeling of harm that might come if you finally decide to indulge in those reluctant goals, take a different approach then. Think of it as what can you be on that other side of the river? What colors does the other side of the canvas have? What laughs can you have if you made that one joke? What gains you can have if you increased just one pound?

If you try to make your fears a medium of self-analysis, maybe you start to gain the motivation that faded quickly with every second you spent in front of that source of fear. Then you might start to see a whole new image of your personality and this might be the person you always wish you could be!

Chapter 3:
There's No Time for Regrets

Regret. Guilt. Shame.

These are three of the darkest emotions any human will ever experience. We all feel these things at different points in our lives, especially after making a "bad" decision. There are certain situations some of us would rewind (or delete) if we could. The reality is, however, there is an infinite number of reasons we should never regret any of the decisions we make in our lives.

Here are 7 of them:

1. Every decision allows you to take credit for creating your own life.

Decisions are not always the result of thoughtful contemplation. Some of them are made on impulse alone. Regardless of the decision, when you made it, it was something you wanted, or you would not have done it (unless someone was pointing a gun at your head).

Be willing to own the decisions you make. Be accountable for them. Take responsibility and accept them.

2. By making any decision involving your heart, you have the chance to create more love in the world by spreading yours.

Your love is a gift.

Once you decide to love, do it without reservation. By fully giving of yourself, you expand your ability to express and receive love. You have added to the goodness of our universe by revealing your heart to it.

3. By experiencing the disappointment that might come with a decision's outcome, you can propel yourself to a new level of emotional evolution.

You aren't doing yourself any favors when you try to save yourself from disappointment. Disappointment provides you with an opportunity to redefine your experiences in life. By refining your reframing skills, you increase your resilience.

4. "Bad" decisions are your opportunity to master the art of self-forgiveness.

When you make a "bad" decision, *you* are the person who is usually the hardest on yourself. Before you can accept the consequences of your decision and move on, you must forgive yourself. You won't always make perfect choices in your life. Acknowledge the beauty in your human imperfection, then move forward and on.

5. Because of the occasional misstep, you enable yourself to live a Technicolor life.

Anger. Joy. Sadness.

These emotions add pigment to your life. Without these things, you would feel soulless. Your life would be black and white.

Make your decisions with gusto. Breathe with fire. You are here to live in color.

6. Your ability to make a decision is an opportunity to exercise the freedom that is your birthright.

How would you feel if you had no say in those decisions concerning your life? Would you feel powerless? Restricted? Suffocated?

Now, focus on what it feels like to make the decisions you want to make. What do you feel? Freedom? Liberty? Independence?

What feelings do you *want* to feel?

Freedom. Liberty. Independence.

As luck would have it, the freedom you want is yours. Be thankful for it in every decision you make, "good" or "bad."

7. When you decide to result in ugly aftermath, you refine what you *do* want in your life.

It's often impossible to know what you want until you experience what you don't want. With every decision, you will experience consequences. Use those outcomes as a jumping-off point to something different (and better) in your future.

Chapter 4:
10 Habits to Change Your Life

I'm sure everyone wonders at a certain point in their life that what is the thing that is stopping them from reaching their goals. It is your bad and unhealthy habits that hold you down. If you want to succeed in life, you need to get rid of these habits and adopt healthy habits to help you in the long run.

Here are 10 healthy habits that will change your life completely if you can adopt them in your daily life:

1. Start Following a Morning Ritual

Everyone has something that they love to do, i.e., things that boost their energy and uplifts their mood. Find one for yourself and do that every morning. It will help you kickstart your day with a bright and cheerful mood. It will also help you to eliminate mental fatigue and stress. You will find yourself super energetic and productive. Let me tell you some morning rituals that you can try and get benefitted from.

- *Eating Healthy:* If you are very passionate about health and fitness, eating healthy as a morning ritual might be a win-win situation for you. You can have a nutritious breakfast every morning. Balance your breakfast with proper amounts of carbs, fats, proteins, etc. It will not only help you in staying healthy but will also help you kickstart your day on a proactive note.

- *Meditating:* Meditation is an excellent way of clearing your mind, enhancing your awareness, and improving your focus. You can meditate for 20 to 30 minutes every morning. Then you can take a nice warm shower, followed by a fresh cup of coffee. Most importantly, meditating regularly will also help you strengthen your immune system, promote emotional stability, and reduce stress.

- *Motivating:* A daily dose of motivation can work wonders for you. When you are motivated, your productivity doubles, and you make the best out of your day. Every morning, you can simply ask yourself questions like, "If it is the last day of your life, what do you want to do?", "What productive thing can I do today to make the best out of the day" "What do I need to do in order to avoid regretting later for having wasted a day?". When you ask yourself questions like these, you are actually instructing your brain to be prepared for having a packed-up and productive day.

- *Writing:* Writing can be a super-effective way of kickstarting your day. When you journal all your thoughts and emotions every day after waking up, it allows you to relieve yourself from all the mental clutter, unlocks your creative side, and sharpens your focus.

- *Working Out:* Working out is a great morning ritual that you can follow every day. When you work out daily, it helps you burn more fat, improves your blood circulation, and boosts your energy level. If you are interested in fitness and health, this is the perfect morning ritual for you. You can do some cardio exercises, or some strength training, or both. Depending on your suitability, create a workout routine for yourself and make sure to stick to that. If you don't stick to your routine, it won't be of much help.

-

2. Start Following the 80/20 Rule

The 80/20 rule states that almost 20% of the tasks you perform are responsible for yielding 80% of the results. It is why you should invest more time in tasks that can give you more significant results instead of wasting your time on tasks that yield little to no results. In this way, you can not only save time but also maximize your productivity. Most importantly, when you see the results after performing those tasks, you will be more motivated to complete the following tasks. After you have finished performing these tasks, now you can quickly move your concentration and focus towards other activities that you need to do throughout your day.

3. Practice Lots of Reading

Reading is a great habit and a great way to stimulate your creativity and gaining more knowledge. When you get immersed in reading, it calms you and improves your focus, almost similar to meditating. If you practice reading before going to bed, you are going to have a fantastic sleep. You can read non-fiction books, which will help you seek motivation, develop new ideas, and broaden your horizon. You can also get a lot of advice about how to handle certain situations in life.

4. Start Single-tasking

Multitasking is hard, and almost 2% of the world's total population can do this properly. You can try multitasking occasionally. If you keep on trying to do this all the time, it will form a mental clutter, and as a result, your brain won't be able to filter out unnecessary information. Many studies have suggested that it can severely damage your cognitive control and lower your efficiency when you multitask a lot. It is the main reason why you should try to do single-tasking more than multitasking. Prepare a list of all the tasks you need to perform in a day and start with the most important one. Make sure not to rush and to complete one thing at a time.

5. Start Appreciating More

Appreciating things is totally dependent on your mentality. For example, some people can whine and complain about a glass being half empty, whereas some people appreciate that there is half a glass of water. It totally depends on your point of view and way of thinking. People get blinded by the urge to reach success so much that they actually forget to appreciate the little things in life. If you are working and earning a handsome salary, don't just sit and complain about why you are not earning more, what you need to do to achieve that, etc. You should obviously aim high, but not at the cost of your well-being. When you practice gratitude, it increases your creativity, improves your physical health, and reduces your stress. You can start writing about the things you are grateful for in your journal every day before going to bed, make some time for appreciating your loved ones, or remind yourself of all the things you are grateful for before going to bed every day. If you are not happy with your current situation, you will not be happy in the future. You need to be happy and satisfied at first, and then only you can work on progressing further.

6. Always Keep Positive People Around You

When you have toxic people around you, it gets tough for you to stay in a good mood or achieve something good in life. Toxic people always find a way to pull you down and make you feel bad about yourself. You should always surround yourself with people who are encouraging and positive. When you do that, your life is going to be full of positivity.

7. Exercise on a Regular Basis

Start exercising regularly to maintain good health and enhancing your creativity and cognitive skills. It also increases your endurance level and boosts your energy. When you exercise regularly, your body produces more endorphins. These hormones work as anti-depressants.

8. Start Listening More

Effective communication is very important in maintaining both professional and personal relationships. For communicating effectively, you need to work on your listening capability first. You need to pay attention to the things said by others instead of focusing only on what you have to say. Listening to others will allow you to understand them better. When you listen to someone, it makes them understand that they are valued and that you are here to listen to them. When they feel important and valued, they also start paying attention to what you say, thereby contributing to effective communication. Don't try to show fake concentration while you are busy thinking about something else. When you listen more, you learn more.

9. Take a Break from Social Media (Social Media Detox)

Many studies have shown that excessive use of social media can contribute to depression. Most importantly, it wastes a lot of time because people meaninglessly scroll, swipe, and click for hours. It is a very unhealthy habit and is very bad for bothe physical and mental health. Sometimes you need to completely stop using social media for a while to reduce mental clutter and stress. Turn off your laptops and phones every day for a few hours. It will help you to reconnect with the surrounding world and will uplift your mood.

10. Start Investing More in Self-care

Make some time for yourself out of your busy schedule. It is going to boost your self-esteem, improve your mental health, and uplift your mood. You need to do at least one thing for yourself every day that will make you feel pampered and happy. You can prepare a mouth-watering meal, take a comfortable bubble bath, learn something new, or just relax while listening to music.

The moment you start introducing these habits in your daily, you will instantly see change. Remember that even a tiny step towards a positive change can give outstanding results if you stay consistent.

Chapter 5:
6 Triggers That Make New Habits Stick

Character development does not stop at developing new habits. It also includes making them stick to form your personality. Overhauling a person's personality is not a walk in the park. This explains why many people are unable to stick to their New Year resolutions of adopting new desirable habits.

You may shift the blame of your failure of permanently adopting new progressive habits from one reason to another. To succeed, it has to be a self-initiative to make things work for you.

These six triggers make new habits stick:

1. <u>Change Your Company</u>

Bad company ruins good morals. This life lesson is true even when people try to convince themselves otherwise. Your circle of friends determines your behavior. They are powerful to turn your personality inside out. The habits of the company you keep will most likely infect you and before you know it, you will start behaving like them.

When you have decided to adopt new habits contrary to those of your friends, you will fail if you retain their company. You have to dissociate with them for the new habits you adopt to stick. In their place, find like-minded friends with whom you share a common purpose.

2. Practice Persistently

You should regularly practice the new habit you desire to adopt for it to stick. Practice makes perfect. You become used to a new habit if it forms part of your routine. With time, the habit no longer becomes tedious but enjoyable. You get to embrace it more and before you know it, it has found its place in your lifestyle.

If you want to develop a reading habit, ensure you read some literature daily. Intentionally select the genre of literature that thrills you and read continuously not just when it is convenient. The effort and practice you put towards this will make the reading habit stick permanently.

3. Set Alarms and Reminders

Alarms and reminders are a constant signal calling you out to attend to something you had dedicated time to do. We set alarms, reminders, or both to make us remember our dedication to doing a task we intended. They are vital to holding us accountable for a decision we made.

Omnipresence is a trait human beings lack. Reminders do the due diligence of not letting you forget to do something you intended and scheduled time for. When you set alarms to remind you to do something, you will always remember it. With time, an alarm becomes unnecessary because the new habit would have stuck and formed your routine.

4. Learn More About The New Habit

Knowledge is power. When you seek knowledge on a new habit that you intend to adopt and make it stick, you understand how easy or difficult your journey shall be. This makes you prepared for any eventuality. When you face difficulty when things get tough, it does not come as a surprise and you will soldier on to continue with your new habit.

Your insight into the new habits you want to make stick is important because it will inform how you relate with your family and friends. Moreover, you get to be more effective in adopting these habits unlike when an ignorant person tries adopting the same.

5. <u>Be Disciplined</u>

Discipline is the glue that guarantees your commitment. The lack of it seals your failure towards any cause you set your heart to. When you are undisciplined, you will overlook many things that contribute to your success in making a habit stick. Introducing a foreign habit into your lifestyle is a tedious task if you lack the discipline to keep you going.

Indiscipline is responsible for many failed missions. You have to be a disciplined person to succeed in anything. It cannot apply selectively. When you pass the discipline test, the new habits you adopt shall stick. To aid you to have discipline, penalize yourself whenever you fail in something. Consequences will enable you to adopt new habits successfully.

6. <u>Be Self-Driven</u>

Habits that sprout from within are more likely to stick compared to those instilled in us by authorities. People adhere to the latter more than they do to the former. It is paramount that the drive to adopt a new habit be a self-driven initiative because you will follow it.

There is rebellion and resistance if people take on certain habits by force or if they do out of fear of the possible ramifications that they might face. You have to first love a habit and purpose to practice it for you to be successful in making it stick in your lifestyle.

In conclusion, these six triggers will make new habits stick only if you apply them correctly.

Chapter 6:

10 Habits to Start Right Now

Have you ever wondered why you are not able to achieve your goals and aspirations? You might get a little confused while searching for the stumbling block on the way to your success, but the answer is simple and right in front of you. It is procrastination and some other unhealthy habits.

Here are ten healthy habits that you need to start incorporating in your life immediately.

1. Maintaining a Routine

You can't expect that everything will be in order one fine morning and you will start achieving all your goals suddenly just like that. It doesn't work that way. Success comes when you start taking small steps every day and slowly work on your progress little by little. You need to start to maintain a routine regularly. Doing this will help you get rid of your procrastination. You can start with simple things like doing some household chores like cooking, cleaning, etc. Let's say you have decided to cook every day – whenever you think that you need to cook all three meals and for everyone, it might intimidate you. You can start with small tasks that are more manageable. So, start with cooking an item every day. That won't take much time and won't be that difficult either – once you start doing this, start increasing the amount and intensity of the work. After you understand how this routine thing works, you can slowly move towards the work related to your goals and aspirations and maintain a routine.

2. Embracing Immediacy

Most people like to put things aside for doing those later. It is a huge mistake that can have serious consequences. People procrastinate everything like problematic things, easy things, small things, big things, and fun things. When you put aside something for doing it later, it gets more challenging to do with time. So, you just keep pushing it further and further until there is no time left to do it. You can overcome this by immediacy. Whenever you are reminded or informed about some work, start doing it immediately and don't keep it pending for later. If it is a small thing that requires a little time to finish, then make sure to finish it in one go. If it is a long work, start working immediately and take breaks and work whenever possible.

3. React Thoughtfully

Most people allow their emotions to control their reactions. Try to avoid making decisions while your emotions are heightened. This is because the decisions that are taken while emotions are heightened are usually wrong decisions and can have detrimental consequences. Your heightened emotions make you blind, and you do things that you wouldn't have done otherwise. So, whenever something triggers you, don't let your gut reaction out. Wait for some time, probably 5-6 minutes, and then act. When you give yourself a little time, it allows you to see through the situation and think beyond those overwhelming emotions. It will make you see the bigger picture and react thoughtfully.

4. Quitting Clicks, Swipes, and Scrolls

Do you even realize how much time you spend aimlessly clicking, swiping, or scrolling? It wastes a lot of your time and is also responsible for draining your productivity, concentration, and motivation. A little bit of digital media does no harm. It is, in fact, helpful because you can get loads of information from the media. But if you keep scrolling for hours, that is where the problem begins. You need to cut down on your use of media to allow yourself to get benefitted from it. If you find difficulty reducing the use of media by yourself, you can try using a browser blocker. It will block all the media outlets after a specified amount of time, thereby limiting the time you spend over there.

5. Embracing the Old

It is usual for people to crave new things every time. But sometimes, people get so overwhelmed by the excitement of trying to gain something new that they forget to cherish the things they already have in their possession. Gaining something you wanted to can be a little exciting and fun for some time, but this will just feed your urge to gain more and more things. Most people already possess everything they require, but they don't seem to see it because of the urge to get something new. For example, a person having a closet full of clothes keeps on buying new clothes every time he has somewhere to go. If you find yourself in a similar situation, you can avoid this by looking at the closet carefully and observing everything you have in your possession. You can, maybe, rearrange the closet in a way where you will be able to see stuff the way you want to see. Once you start cherishing the things that you already have, you can go a long way.

6. Remember Your Achievements

Sometimes, you are too harsh on yourself, and you blame yourself way too much. You should always treat yourself with the same amount of kindness and positivity you possess while treating others. Everyone has their fair share of successes and failures in their lives. So, you should be grateful for everything you achieved and not take those for granted. Instead of regretting and blaming yourself for the things you couldn't achieve, try reminding yourself amount the things you actually did achieve. Appreciate yourself for every good thing that you have done in your life. It can be something like quitting certain habits, scoring certain marks in an exam, doing something good for others, etc. So, whenever you make some mistake, you need to remind yourself of all the small and big things you have achieved so that you don't get too disheartened to get up and move on. Embrace the good in you!

7. Declutter

Have you ever felt that whenever you change the orientation of the furniture in your room, you get excited and feel different? This is because even a tiny change is considered to be new, fun, and exciting. Your motivation and productivity get hugely affected by your workspace environment. If your workspace environment is messy, it is going to inspire your creativity subconsciously. In contrast, if you have a well-organized workspace, it will subconsciously boost your efficiency and help you remove any mental clutter. Keep changing your workspace from time to time. Keep it messy somedays, for increasing your creativity levels. When you need to do a lot of hard work that demands efficiency, arrange everything in order and make your workspace well-organized. You can add some photo frames to give it a different and exciting look.

8. Set Small Achievable Goals Everyday

People feel the most satisfied when they know that they have achieved a certain goal. You can use it to your advantage for brightening up your day. Set small achievable goals throughout your day so that you can easily achieve them. It can be as simple as making your bed after you get up, and so on. Make sure that you already have 2-3 achieved goals before you have your breakfast. These small benchmarks play a vital role in kick-starting your day on a good note. All these little benchmarks add up and give you a sense of pride and satisfaction after you achieve them, thereby brightening up your day.

9. Give Compliments

People love to receive compliments from others but get a little shaky while giving compliments to others. Have you ever wondered why? It is probably because you worry about how it would make you look like. You feel that complimenting others can make you look lighter and easy. That's absolutely not the case. Complimenting people can really help you start a conversation with different people and get friendly. It is a fantastic social skill that you need to learn because of the various benefits it offers. Don't fear what others will think, and don't sugarcoat your words either. Because when you give fake compliments, people can feel that it is not coming from your heart, leaving a very negative impression on them. Try to be as genuine as possible and speak your mind out.

10. Commit to Relaxation

A lot of people work continuously, and even when they are taking a break, all they think about is their work! It is not a healthy habit and needs to be changed immediately. When you work yourself too much and don't give yourself the amount of relaxation it deserves, work seems to be more complicated than it actually is, thereby reducing your productivity and concentration. When you feel like you can't work anymore and that you have reached your threshold cut yourself some slack! When you are taking a break, make sure not to think about work at all. Plan something relaxing, exciting, or fun, and enjoy yourself fully while taking some time off from your work. It will recharge your mind, and then you can return to your work, being energetic and positive.

I hope you follow these steps and develop them as habits in your daily life so that you can make the most out of your life and stay happy.

Chapter 7:
5 Habits of Bill Gates

Bill gates is a name synonymous with success. Who does not know Bill Gates? His footprints are everywhere. Students in elementary school look up to him as their role model. Those in high school and higher levels of education idolize him. He is a semi-god, everyone wanting to identify himself or herself with his success.

Well, here are 5 habits of Bill Gates:

1. He Is Generous

The 65-year-old founder of Microsoft Corporation is by no means a mean person (pun intended). He has donated to charity drives uncountable times. Many students are beneficiaries of his generosity through the Bill & Melinda Gates Foundation. He has come out strongly to support the education of black and Latino students, and those experiencing poverty in the United States.

Bill Gates – co-chair and trustee of Bill & Melinda Gates Foundation – has committed over $1.75 billion over two years for Covid-19 pandemic relief. He, besides Mackenzie Scott, Warren Buffet, and George Soros are among the wealthiest most generous people.

He understands perfectly that to him who much is given, much will be expected. The world is full of praises for the generosity of the world's fourth-richest person. His foundation is the world's largest charitable foundation and he has not stopped at that. To the father of three, poverty eradication is one of his life-long goals.

We can take a cue from him and start giving to receive. We should not always be the recipients of charities. Learn to give, not out of abundance but out of the love for humanity.

2. He Treasures His Family

It is an open secret that the father of three is a family man. It is amazing how he has been able to keep his family together all those years despite his wealth. Until May 4th 2021, Bill was married to Melinda. In a statement sent to the BBC, they said it was regrettable that they had to end their 27-year-old marriage. Nevertheless, his contribution to keeping his family close to his chest cannot be ignored.

He has not allowed his family affairs to come out to the public. Even when he divorced his wife in May 2021, they issued a joint statement to the media and kept their divorce under wraps. This is unlike the noisy and messy divorces that most celebrities have.

We learn from Bill Gates the importance of family. It is always God first and family next. Treasure your family because blood is always thicker than water. Whenever there is conflict, do not let it spill out to the public but sort it out amicably.

3. He Is A Social Man

From public appearances in social functions to corporate events, Bill Gates does not shy away from the public. He takes his time to attend personally to matters that require his presence. He has learned not to build a fortress or isolate himself.

With the type of publicity he receives, a man of his stature would naturally want to lead a quiet life and focus primarily on his businesses. However, he has a strong online presence. Be it LinkedIn, Twitter, Instagram, or Facebook, he shares his thoughts fearlessly.

Moreover, the technology giant founder engages captains of industry in meaningful and fruitful conversations. He has embraced the human nature of socializing and talking to people. Likewise, we should follow in tow. We should not live in fortresses because we will be cut off from the outside world and that will be the beginning of our downfall.

Attend that lunch or dinner with your colleagues, go to the graduation party of your associates, attend birthday parties and weddings. It is these social events and more that will link you with potential destiny connectors and you will grow your network. Your network is your net worth.

4. He Is Conscious of His Public Image

Bill Gates has created for himself an image of a calm and composed leader. Dressed in smart elegant suits for every occasion, the multi-billionaire never fails to impress. Not once can you fault the man over his dress code. Have you ever heard of the saying "dress how you want to be addressed?"

Your dressing speaks volumes as to the kind of person you are. Dressing in itself is an art. Carefully observe not to underdress or overdress because it sends an unspoken message to those you meet.

Never has the 65-year-old billionaire been involved in a public saga. He is careful to carry himself with decorum whenever he is in public. Public perception is key to maintain his social stature – an art he has perfected over the years. Even the speech he gives is in tandem with his public image.

The thought that Bill Gates can speak rumors or even argue in public is unfathomable. He is a towering icon of success and is careful not to belittle his image. It takes a lifetime to build a reputation but a few minutes to ruin it completely.

5. He Has A Progressive Mindset

It all begins from the mind. Our mindset is what makes us stand out. It is easier for Bill Gates to be content with what he has achieved so far. He made history as the youngest American billionaire at 31 years until Zuckerberg broke that record in 2010.

He has received numerous accolades and awards for his work, but he is still not content at that level. This does not mean that Bill is ungrateful. He is grateful. It is only that he has set his mind on much higher targets. That is the progressive mindset all of us ought to emulate.

Most people fall into the trap of settling down for less in the name of being altruistic. It is time to stop getting comfortable and borrow a page from the lifestyle of Bill. The mind is where reason is born. Bill Gates knows this perfectly well and despite his wealth and achievements, he keeps moving forward.

Bill's progressive mindset has made him grow his corporation to become the world's biggest company with a valuation of $1 trillion. It begins and ends with the mind.

The above are 5 habits of Bill Gates that he has developed over time. They have made him who he is today.

Chapter 8:
<u>*The Goal Is Not The Point*</u>

If you ever want to achieve your goals, stop thinking about them. I know this goes against everything anyone has ever said about achieving your goals.

Everyone says that think about one thing and then stick to it. Devote yourself to that one single goal as you are committed to your next breath. Check on your goals over and over again to see if you are still on track or not and you will get there sooner than you think.

What I am proposing is against all the theories that exist behind achieving your goals but wait a minute and listen to me.

The reason behind this opposing theory is that we spend more time concentrating on thinking and panning about our goals. Rather than actually doing something to achieve them.

We think about getting into college. Getting a Bachelor's degree and then getting our Master's degree and so on. So that we can finally decide to appear for an interview that we have dreamed about or to start a business that we are crazy about.

But these are not the requirements for any of them to happen. You can get a degree in whatever discipline you want or not, and can still opt for business. As far as job interviews are concerned, they are not looking for the most educated person for that post. But the most talented and experienced person that suits the role on hand.

So we purposefully spend our life doing things that carry the least importance in actual to that goal.

What we should be doing is to get started with the simplest things and pile upon them as soon as possible. Because life is too short to keep thinking.

Thinking is the easiest way out of our miseries. Staying idol and fantasizing about things coming to reality is the lamest thing to do when you can actually go out and start discovering the opportunities that lie ahead of you.

Your goals are things that are out of your control. You might get them, you might not. But the actions, motivation, and the effort you put behind your goal make the goal a small thing when you actually grab it. Because then you look back and you feel proud of yourself for what you have achieved throughout the journey.

At the end of that journey, you feel happier and content with what you gained within yourself irrespective of the goal. Because you made yourself realize your true potential and your true purpose as an active human being.

Find purpose in the journey for you can't know for sure about what lies ahead. But what you do know is that you can do what you want to do to your own limits. When you come to realize your true potential, the original goal seems to fade away in the background. Because then your effort starts to appear in the foreground.

A goal isn't always meant to be achieved as it might not be good for you in the end or in some other circumstances. But the efforts behind these goals serve as something to look back on and be amazed at.

Chapter 9:
<u>10 Habits of Jeff Bezos</u>

As you know, your lifestyle choices can make or break your success. It began in a basement and has since grown into a well-known online shopping app. Jeff Bezos' brainchild, the "Everything Store," is a platform where people get online deals. Commonly known as Amazon.com, the "Everything Store" is billion dollars' worth.

Jeff Bezos' habits vary from what to read to dealing with stress, which he phrases as "laugh a lot." Bezos, the self-made millionaire and Amazon CEO, is one of the world's wealthiest persons. But, what got him there? His natural aptitude for business got him there. Moreover, his habits are key to his achievements.

Here are ten business-oriented Jeff Bezos' habits for innovative-minds upkeep.

1. **Customer-Centric Approach**

Unlike most of the business, Bezos and Amazon have in decades ignored a "profitable" approach to doing business; instead, he invests in a customer-centric approach. Although at some point Amazon got chastised by publishers for allowing the laity to evaluate books, Amazon encouraged its consumers to share their comments, whether critical or negative.

An incentive that created a Clientele review platform which is why Amazon.com is today's most trusted e-commerce platform. Keeping a soundtrack of your customers means that you're taking good care of them.

2. Make Your Plan Based on Things That Will Not Change

While trading your brands-be it, lipstick, tractor seats, e-book readers, or data storages, make bigger plans with these constants: Provider your clientele with a broader selection scope, lower pricing, and rapid, dependable delivery.

3. Create Your Own Rules

If you despise writing essays, Amazon might not be the place for you. Amazon made it a rule early that anyone who wishes to suggest a new concept must first condense their views into a six-page booklet.
Before making any decisions, everyone concerned, must read and analyze the six-pager. And also, according to Bezos, "no team should be so large that two pizzas won't be enough." When your organization is far larger to be fed by two pizzas, divide it into fewer independent units of your own liking and capabilities to compete for limited resources while making your customers happy.

4. Work Backwards to What Your Customers Require

Customers' desires, rather than drivers' preferences, have shaped the specifications for Amazon's significant new projects, such as the Kindle tablets and e-book readers. So if your clientele doesn't want something, let it go, even if it means dismantling a once-powerful department.

5. Master the Art of Failure

Bezos's Amazon recruited many editors to produce book and music evaluations but later decided to use user feedback instead. A move that failed miserably.

Such blunders, according to Bezos, are a normal part of your innovative life, as long as you're on a learning reality, failure is sometimes positive. To succeed as an innovator, means that you are in for such flaws as taking risks, failing at a point while tucking your sleeves for a changes.

6. Make Informed Choices or Decisions

If you did know that Amazon began as a bookstore, well, here you have it! Bezos' product decisions are always a product of well thought logics and factual data rather than incidental incentives. Your product decision should be knowledgeable, and reading is knowledge.

In a nutshell, books are the ideal driver for e-commerce. Because nearly every aspect of commerce and customer behavior can be quantified, and almost all choices are based on data. Meetings are about metrics, not tales from customers!

7. You Are Willing To Be Misinterpreted for a Long Time

Many of Bezos-Amazon's initiatives appear as money-losing distractions. Which severally send the company's stock price down and earns the wrath of focal analysts. A five-to-seven-year financial plan is acceptable if your new initiatives make strategic sense to you.

8. Don't Mind the Competition

If your business is imitating and engrossed in what others are doing, then you're off Jeff Bezos' innovative strategies. In truth, client service should always come first. Just as Amazon Prime, succeed in your innovative plans while satisfying your clientele-base.

9. Don't Try To Be a Blockbuster

Your present success does not guarantee your future relevance. Consider the fate of Blockbuster Video and accept the fact that your industry advances with time, and will never hold similar standing as of now. Pay close attention to evolving state of affairs as you lead the change rather than reacting to it.

10. Ditch Complexity

Startups are characterized by rapid decision-making and innovation. However, as a company grows, it is frequently delayed by complexity. This suffocates innovation. Just like Bezos, always treat your company as a start-up at the cutting edge.

Conclusion

Following Jeff Bezos uniqueness will not guarantee you $100 billion. But you'll still set yourself up for a more prosperous future with your company endeavors if you maintain this proactive, forward-thinking approach.

Chapter 10:
5 Habits For An Extremely Productive Day

Our productivity and efficiency during the day are variables of several factors. Some days seem better, the sun a little brighter than normal; the food tastes sweeter and the mood lighter. In such days, unmatched joy bubbles within us increasing our productivity exponentially. Many people cannot choose when to experience these days. Instead, they are at the mercy of their emotions and the influence of other people who can ruin their day whenever they please.

Here are five habits for an extremely productive day:

1. <u>Plan For Your Day Beforehand.</u>

Failure to plan is planning to fail. A plan is an integral part of success. It means that you understand the obligation you have to live the day ahead and the duties and responsibilities in your in-tray. A plan will help you check all the boxes on your to-do list and you can track your progress in each.

In planning for your day, you will know the resources that you have and those that you lack. It is also possible to budget on your means earlier rather than waiting for the actual day and start scampering for resources. A wise man does not live on a borrowed budget but within his own.

A good plan is a job half done. Your day will be more productive when nothing takes you by surprise because you would have anticipated every occurrence beforehand and it will find you armed with a solution.

2. <u>Wake Up Early</u>

The early bird catches the worm. Punctuality is very important if you want to have a productive day. An early riser has a fresh and clear mind compared to those who wake up late and start their routine fast because they are behind schedule. They do not have the advantage of calmness and composure because they want to make up for time lost. This exposes them to error and ridicule from their enemies if they fail, which is imminent because of their inaccuracy.

When one wakes up early, one has an advantage over other people. They can open their businesses or start their work earlier than their competitors do. They maximize their productivity because they have created enough time for each task they had scheduled. Consider waking up early to have an extremely productive day.

3. <u>Do Not Bite More Than You Can Chew</u>

This calls for sobriety in the handling of tasks and designing of goals. The pressure to outdo yourself can be overwhelming enough to make you lose focus on what is at stake. It is paramount to set realistic and achievable goals so that you can concentrate on them. Shun anything that presents itself to you that is beyond your ability no matter how attractive it seems.

The power of self-control is at play. Resist the temptation of going out of your way to prove a point for the sake of it. Instead, fully concentrate on what you had planned. Schedule anything outside your plan to the following day. It is far from procrastination because in this case, you have a clearly defined timeline on when to actualize your plans.

Failure to develop this habit will lead you to a situation where you have many unfinished tasks. This is not productivity, by all standards. Focus on what you can manage and do it efficiently.

4. Avoid Negative Company

A negative company will derail your progress and work. When you associate yourself with such people, you will not see the unseen benefit in challenges and instead, you will focus on the undone, incomplete, and failed bits of your work. Failure is contagious. If you constantly surround yourself with a clique of failures, you too shall fail.

To have a productive day, have friends who share your vision. You will blossom under their shade and they will encourage you in your work. This will show you possibility even when you see failure and doom. In their company, your days will be productive and joyful.

5. Look At The Bigger Picture

As you seek to have productive days, look at the bigger picture. It will make you focus on the greater plan you have rather than petty squabbles and meaningless distractions that come your way. The bigger picture will always remind you of your cause and inspire you to live up to it even when challenges come your way.

When you pay attention to the above five habits, you will have extremely productive days. It all lies in your effort to adopt them.

Chapter 11:
10 Habits of Bernard Arnault

Bernard Arnault- French investor, businessman, and CEO of LVMH recently reclaimed the title "worlds' wealthiest" from fellow billionaire Jeff Bezos. His business acumen and awe-inspiring financial achievements deserve to be recognized. His perspective can serve as a model for entrepreneurs who want to follow in his footsteps.

Bernard Arnault has written about money, prosperity, leadership, and power over the years. Moreover, his path to becoming the CEO of one of the world's most recognized brands will provide you with valuable lessons to emulate from. That is, your life circumstances shouldn't stop you from expanding and thriving outside your expertise.

Following his impressive accomplishments, here are ten points you can take away from Arnault's journey to success.

1. **Happiness Before Money**

According to Bernard, happiness is leading. That is leading your team to the top whether you are in business, sports, music industry. Money, according to him, is a consequence, and success is a blend of your past and future.

Your priority is not what you'll make sooner! When you put much-required effort into your job, profits will flow.

2. Mistakes Your Lesson

Your biggest mistake is your learning opportunity. When your business isn't performing well, understand the situation first and be patient.

In the world of innovative brands, it can take years to get something to work. Give it time and put yourself in a long-term expectation.

3. Always Behave as a Startup

Think small. Act quickly. Smaller boats can turn faster than more giant tankers. Arnault emphasizes the significance of thinking small. LVMH, in Arnault's opinion, is not a massive corporation device with miles of unnecessary bureaucracy.

Believe in your vision while attracting the best talent for your success path. A handy, adaptable speed, one that can fail quickly as easy to sleeve up.

4. Continuously Reinvent Yourself

How do you maintain your relevance? Bernard's LVMH is built on innovation, quality, entrepreneurship, and, essentially, on long-term vision. LVMH excels at developing increasingly desirable new products and selling them globally.

To be successful today, with your capabilities, opt for a worldwide startup and see what's going on. This necessitates a more considerable investment, which gives you an advantage. However, let the Creators run your inventions.

5. Team-Creative Control

Arnault strategies find creative control under each product's team to do what they do best. Arnault's designers are the dreamer's realists and critics. Allow your team to take creative control. You risk putting a tourniquet around their minds if you restrict them in any way.

6. Create Value To Attract Customers

Marketing investigates what the customer desires. As a result, you are doing what they need: creating a product and testing it to see if it works. Keeping your products in close contact with consumers, according to Arnault, makes a desire to buy in them. LVMH creates products that generate customers. For him, it's never about sales; it's always about creating desire. Your goal should be to be desirable for long-term marketability.

7. Trust the Process

There will always be different voices in business, and while there will undoubtedly be good advice, if you believe an idea will succeed, you may need to persevere until the end. Like Arnault, disregard your critics by following through with your vision to excel.

8. Your Persistence Is Everything

It would be best if you were very persistent. It would be best to have ideas, but the idea is only 20% of the equation. The execution rate is 80%. So if you are trying out a startup, having ideas marvellous, the driving force is persistence and execution.

When it comes to the most successful startups, such as Facebook, the idea was great from the beginning. Others, however, had the same idea. So why is Facebook such a phenomenal success today? It is critically through execution with persistence.

9. **Do Not Think of Yourself**

Bernard Arnault can be differentiated from other billionaires like Elon Musk or Bill Gates by focusing on the brands, making their longevity rather than making himself the face. He is only concerned with promoting his products.

To accomplish this, you must maintain contact with pioneers and designers, for example, while also making their ideas more specific and sustainable.

10. **Maintain Contact With Your Company**

One of the most common leadership mistakes is to lose sight of the company once you reach the top and "stick" with manageable goals. Instead, to see if the machine is working correctly or if there is room for improvement, you must examine every corner and every part of it.

Conclusion

Your willingness to outwork and your ability to outlearn everyone will keep your success journey intact and going. Bernard Arnault's path to becoming the CEO of the worlds most recognized and desired multi-billion empire of brands have a valuable lesson for you: your starting point does not influence or determine your future destination.

Chapter 12:
10 Habits of Successful Traders

Becoming a successful trader is the dream of every business person. It is the crux of the art of doing business and only a handful of traders attain it. Trade has its ups and downs and a lot is required of you if you are to make it.

Here are ten habits of successful traders:

1. <u>They Are Well Connected</u>

Connections could be just what you are lacking for you to have that boom you have yearning. Doing business in urban areas is not a walk in the park. Successful traders seek partnerships with celebrities who help them market their products or services.

When you have a good relationship with influential people, they will channel customer traffic your way. Businesses with public figures as their brand ambassadors are more likely to do well in a highly competitive industry.

2. <u>They Are Good Managers</u>

Successful traders believe in themselves managing their trade. It is very difficult to find an unsupervised trustworthy employee who will steer a business to success. This has made successful traders learn to manage their business even if they were armatures at the beginning.

Over time, they manage to perfect their management skills and require external help less often. Management requires practice and successful traders do not give up learning it. Some even enroll in colleges to learn management skills that they will implement in their businesses.

3. <u>They Are Risk-Takers</u>

The art of doing trade sometimes requires extreme decisions involving risks. The return on investment of risky ventures is high, although few traders are ready to wade into such territories. This makes only a handful of traders successful.

Taking calculated risks is the habit of successful traders. They have a backup mechanism to cushion their businesses in the event of an unanticipated loss. The underlying principle in investment is that the higher the risk the higher the returns.

4. <u>They are Knowledgeable About Their Market</u>

Knowledge is power and successful traders use this tool in their businesses. You need accurate and precise information about the market if you want to meet its needs. Successful traders do not sit back to wait for information but instead hunt for it themselves.

With the right data, they implement the right strategies. Unlike merchants who are in business aimlessly, successful traders have relevant information about the market they operate in at their fingertips.

5. <u>They Take Customer Feedback Seriously</u>

Feedback is an important aspect of communication. Serious traders end up successful because they incorporate this in their businesses. They always seek client responses on how they enjoyed their goods or services. Routine asking for feedback is not in vain. It is aimed at improving their services or products for consumer consumption. When clients observe that their feedback was taken seriously, they will be motivated to use their products once more. Feedback is very powerful in sealing the success of any trade.

6. They Conform To The Emerging Trends

The needs of the market are ever-evolving and those in business should learn to evolve with them. This is a common habit of successful traders. They will go the extra mile to provide a new service to meet market demand.

The success of traders in competitive sectors of the economy is pegged on their adapting to new styles. They will be the first to stock clothes in fashion or the latest mobile devices. It is such stock that will move fast and they will realize higher revenues.

7. They Are Patient

Sometimes business could be at a low season. This does not qualify the traders to quit the business. Like everything else, business too has its off-peak days. Great patience is needed to survive this season – a trait successful traders have no shortage of.

Patience is required to grow a business steadily through the stages of growth until it breaks even and starts earning profit. Thereafter, the same business will pass the ceiling and register huge profit margins.

8. They Rarely Give Credit

As much as traders may want to give credit to maintain customer loyalty, the success of a business may not be realized if they overdo it. There are several factors that successful business people consider before allowing credit and being reckless about it is not one of them.

Customer loyalty is not guaranteed because you allow credit. It may make you be bankrupt and close shop. Successful traders give discounts when their clients make purchases instead of giving credit recklessly.

9. They Maintain An Excellent Relationship With Their Suppliers

The relationship between traders and their suppliers is as equally important as that between them and their customers. Successful traders build bridges with their suppliers over time even up to the point of getting goods on credit to sell and pay later.

Such strong relationships with suppliers ensure these traders never run out of stock. Customers will always find goods from their stores and business will run smoothly. This makes a great difference in trade to crown them successful.

10. They Are Law-Abiding

Trade is legitimate in all jurisdictions worldwide except that the items of trade are illegal in that country. This informs the success of a business. It should conform to existing laws and be subject to inspection by authorities.

Successful traders are law-abiding. They pay taxes and seek a license to operate. This insulates their businesses from legal action against them. Their acceptance of regulation will help them remain open when their peers are evading crackdowns on illicit trade. They attract more customers because of their consistency in operation.

In conclusion, successful traders are tied to the hip by these ten habits. They have propelled them to their success. To be successful like they are, implement them and watch your star in trade rise.

Chapter 13:
Ten habits of David Beckham

David Robert Joseph Beckham, famously known as only David Beckham, was born on 2nd May 1975 in Leytonstone, East London, England to Ted and Sandra Beckham. He is the only son in his family between two sisters. His family members were staunch fans of Manchester United. He showed interest in football while he was still a child and started charting his path as a professional soccer player.

Here are ten habits of David Beckham:

1. He is a great leader.

David is a great leader both in the pitch and outside. He was the England national team captain from 2000 to 2006. During his tenure, he led England to the World Cup in 2002 and 2006. He singlehandedly scored against Greece to qualify England for the World Cup in 2002.

The Briton soccer star addressed the Discovery Leadership Summit in Johannesburg in 2016. He was among key speakers in the summit themed on leadership in business, government, and civil society.

2. He is philanthropic.

Beckham is involved in many charity drives. He has been the goodwill ambassador of the United Nations Children's Fund (UNICEF) since 2005. He champions the good welfare of children globally campaigning on issues affecting children like malnutrition, emergencies, child violence, and abuse.

He founded 7: The David Beckham UNICEF Fund that has changed the lives of vulnerable children globally. He has a personal commitment to secure the future of children and woo world leaders to his cause.

3. <u>He knows when and where to stop.</u>

The former football legend knows his limits and how to make things work for him. He voluntarily retired from playing professional football in May 2013 after 21 years in the game. David understood when to take a break in his career and venture into other activities.

He resisted the temptation of adding an extra year to his contract at Paris Saint-Germain. He was thankful to the French club for allowing him to play for them until the time that he was leaving.

4. <u>He values family.</u>

Beckham adores family ties above everything else. In his retirement speech, he appreciated his family for their sacrifice and support in realizing his dreams. This shows the connection between David and his family.

David said that he owes everything to his wife and children for inspiring him to play for a very long time. Family is most definitely at the heart of the former football icon.

5. <u>He is a businessman.</u>

Apart from soccer, Beckham has ventured into other businesses. He co-owns Beckham brand holdings and Kent & Curwen. These businesses have made him worth over $500 million. He ranks among the wealthiest sportsmen in England.

His retirement from paid soccer has made him engage fully in his businesses. He launched an underwear line for H&M in 2012 and modeled wearing them. They are sold in stores in 40 countries worldwide.

6. He is patriotic.

David Beckham has traveled vastly across the world but he has always maintained his fidelity to his country. He started playing football in England's Manchester United youth league and proceeded to its training division before joining the main club as a full-time starter. It was later in his career that he played for Real Madrid, a Spanish team.

He received a royal award – order of British empire – from the queen on 27th November 2003 for his professional services to the nation. The Queen and Beckham exchanged a few words and she told him it was an honor for her to award the British star.

7. He is an investor.

Besides doing business, David Beckham is an investor. He has a 10% stake in Lunaz, a car restoration and electrification firm based in Britain. He is also a co-owner of a virtual sports academy, Guild Esports.

The former English player is an investor in the Major League Soccer (MLS) and invested a further $ 15.3 million to strengthen the team ahead of the second season. He has taken a keen interest in the sport passively after his retirement.

8. <u>He is a good ambassador.</u>

Beckham has partnered with many firms and endorsed their products. His celebrity status has earned him favor with the world and he has many fans who will use the products he uses without question.
According to Forbes, David's sponsors include Adidas, Coty, H&M, Samsung, and Breitling. He was an ambassador for the Chinese super league in 2013. He is an active and competent ambassador for the brands he represents.

9. <u>He loves acting.</u>

Besides his long sports career, David Beckham is also an actor. He has appeared in *Uncle's Man* directed by Ritchie in 2015. He also played the character of Trigger in the famous 2017 movie – *King Arthur: Legend of the sword*.

By his self-admission, he does not take acting as a career but as a hobby. His fans have enjoyed the movies he has acted in and encouraged him to keep on entertaining them.

10. <u>He enjoys public attention.</u>

Beckham has always been intimate with the attention he has been receiving. His life has always been an open book to the world. Fans once thronged him wanting to take selfies with the football legend when he had gone for lunch with Garry Neville and Ryan Giggs.

He enjoyed the attention he received and took photos with his fans before entering his car and leaving the scene. This is expected of him because he has grown up in the public limelight from his childhood to adulthood.

In conclusion, these ten habits of the former English footballer have majorly defined his lifestyle.

Chapter 14:
6 Habits of Ridiculously Likeable People

We all know someone with great influence on everyone he/she meets. They have the ability to change your mind in an instant. You cannot help but love them for who they are. Their charisma is unmatched and their enthusiasm is heavenly. To some, this is innate but to others, they build this character over time.

Here are 6 Habits of Ridiculously Likeable People:

1. <u>They Are Talkative</u>

Most likeable people are talkative. They never tire of talking about their experiences or their thoughts. It appears that they have nothing to hide and you can easily see through their lives. It is not easy to offend them because they say aloud their likes and dislikes even without anyone enquiring. Everyone around them would know what offends the talker in their midst and would keep off that lane.

Do you know that person at the office who would respectfully talk freely without any reservation? His/her colleagues cannot help but love them for who they are. Talkative people are like an open book and those they interact with are not afraid of them because their intentions are clear.

One misfortune that follows talkers is they are prone to attacks from unfriendly quarters. Their openness is a potential target for enemies. If you are a talkative person, beware of the information you give to others. Detailed personal information is not meant for everyone's ears.

Another disadvantage of talkers is that they may not be trusted with classified information because it is unsafe and unsecure with them. They may unintentionally give it away to the enemy.

Above all, talkative people are loveable to a fault. They speak boldly what others may not. They also lighten the gravity of matters if they are the ones to break such news.

2. They Are Friendly

Friendliness charms even the introverts. It is the right step towards developing healthy relationships. Who can afford to be offensive to a friendly person? Being friendly makes you likeable without any pre requisites. If you can hold a conversation with a stranger beyond greetings, then you are warmly receptive.

On the contrary, hostile people are not likeable because they are offensive and sometimes disrespectful. Hostility creates more enemies than friends – a bad environment for businesses and healthy relationships to thrive.

Friendly people easily create more friends wherever they go. They nature their relationships excellently and grow their network exponentially. They give no reason for anyone not to like them and sometimes turn their foes to allies.

3. They Are Happy Always

Happiness can neither be hidden nor faked. Happiness is also contagious. People will naturally want to be around those who add value to their lives. Your value is measured by the impact you have on those around you. Happy people are automatically loveable. How can you fail to love those who give you a dose of joy every day?

It is amazing the power that happy people wield over those they meet. Such influence does not come through coercion. The impact happy people have in the society, in boardrooms or in the pitch is significant. This makes them very pivotal in many matters and as a result, they win the hearts of many people.

The people who are mean and without humor achieve the contrary of what happy people do. They repel their audiences. Instead of winning the hearts of those they meet, they lose even the trust of those already in their fold.

Happy people are peace loving. Peace is the only avenue that happiness can thrive. A microscopic view of the DNA of ridiculously likeable people shows happiness engrained in the peace they enjoy. Everybody loves peace. By extension, that love will overflow to happy people.

4. <u>They Are Charismatic</u>

Charismatic people are charming to a fault. They are positively confident and not boastful in any manner. Such charisma makes them great influencers, drawing a large following. Renowned world leaders have this personality. Former US president, Barack Obama is a perfect example of a charismatic leader.

He is loved globally more even after he left office in 2016. His charity work does is not ignorable. Such charisma makes him ridiculously likeable. To be universally acceptable, cultivate the charismatic personality.

Like everything else, charisma too can be developed under the right conditions. With proportionate zeal, charisma can increase and consume any hate that may arise.

5. They Are Innocent

To be innocent is simply not to be guilty. Likeable people are free from any guilt of whatever form. Innocence is uncommon in the current world. When the world sees innocence, it is awed by it. People are attracted to what is not common. They will love those it sees innocent.

Who will associate with the guilty? None. If you manage to appeal to the public as innocent, you will be likeable by everyone. Innocent people are free from scandals. The perception that the public has on you is the determinant of innocence.

Scandalous individuals do not appeal to the public. How can you attract love from people when all you do is turn their rage towards you?

Innocence is not an act, but a habit. Do not engage in crime or social injustices. Always be at the forefront in condemning social ills. It will not make you any righteous, but it will prove that you champion the right ideals and make you stand out from the crowd that remains silent on injustices.

6. They Are Bold and Decisive

Boldness is making your stand known. It is not being timid. Bold people are loveable. They are loved because they speak out what others are afraid of saying. Their innocence to ills makes them bold to stand up for the weak and disadvantaged.

The public loves people who are uniquely able to handle what most of them cannot. Be clear in your decisions and do not sit on the fence. Ridiculously liked people attained the level of acceptance they enjoy from possibly a public decision they made on a matter of national or global interest. This set them apart and from then, they were marked for greatness.

Have you ever wondered what propelled great personalities to national or global acceptance? Well, the above are six habits of ridiculously liked people.

Chapter 15:
10 Habits of Kobe Bryant

Throughout 20 seasons, the late Kobe Bryant earned a reputation as the greatest basketball player of all time with the Los Angeles Lakers. The six-foot-six shooting guard dominated the court in NBA history, winning five NBA titles, a record of 18 consecutive All-Star Game selections, four All-Star Game MVP Awards, and the Academy Award for Best Animated Short Film, "Dear Basketball."

Bryant's off-court legacy was similarly outstanding, with record earnings for an NBA player, winning investments, and a lucrative shoe deal that increased his net worth to more than $600 million. He was also renowned for his strong work ethic. Highly applauded, you'll find endless stories on his 20-year career work ethics from his teammates, competitors, coaches, and other acquaintances.

Here are 10 Kobe Bryant's habits.

1. His Work Ethics

Kobe Bryant was well-known for having a solid work ethic. If he ever lost a game, he could figure out why and spend extra time improving. Losing a shot for Kobe meant training for hours and days until he couldn't miss it anymore. He was going to train so hard that you wouldn't beat him.

2. Become Obsessive

Kobe not only obsessed on basketball, but also dedicated his energy on becoming the best in every manner. "If you want to be exceptional at something, you have to obsess over it," he once said. That's precisely the mind set you need if you want to be the best in your field. Embrace your obsession, fall in love with the process, and use it to reach heights that others cannot.

3. Mamba Attitude

Kobe was determined to be one of the greatest basketballers at only 13 years of age. He said in an interview that he was inspired by great players like Michael Jordan and Magic Jordan. He would watch them play and wonder, "Can I get to that level?" "i don't know," he could say, "but let's find out." Whether you're starting a business, becoming a great athlete, learning a new skill, or forming a new habit, modelling your habits after someone who has already succeeded will save you the most time and money in the long run.

4. Compete Against Yourself

When you compete with yourself, you put others in the position to keep up with you. Kobe never had this problem because he fought within him to be the type of athlete who could win more after winning his first championship. Throughout his career, he progressed from being the No. 8 Kobe who wanted to win to the No. 24 Kobe who needed to be a leader and a better teammate.

5. Embracing New Abilities

After Kobe retired from sports in 2016, his next focus was on finding ways to inspire the world through diverse stories, characters, and leadership. He pushed and founded multimedia production company Granity Studios, which is 2018, lead to his Academy Award- a Sports Emmy and an Annie Award for his short animated film Dear Basketball. Embracing new skills will keep your legacy going and diversify your abilities in different walks of life.

6. Leaders develop leaders

"I enjoyed testing people and making them uncomfortable," Kobe once said. "That is what leads to introspection, which leads to improvement. I guess you could say I challenged them to be their best selves." On the court, Kobe was a strong, albeit contentious, leader for his team.

7. Handling the Pressure is Everything

When you're under pressure, you're forced to make critical choices and decisions. Sometimes, you'll make the wrong decisions, but that what keeps you going strong. When Kobe was playing against the Utah Jazz at 18 years, he missed a shot which led to his team losing the game. This had him working on the shot during the entire off-season.

8. Perseverance

Kobe's success was as a result of sticking to his process through perseverance. He was determined not to give in to anyone or anything that pushed him backwards. Your strength to keep moving will eventually payoff.

9. Failure Begets Growth

Failure is only ideal when you keep learning. In an interview, Kobe mentioned being an 11-year-old basketball player who played in a summer league for an entire season without scoring a single point! Really?! So he had to work extra for the following ten months to become a better shot and learn how to score.

10. Passion Is Everything

It's undeniable that Kobe had a strong love and enthusiasm for basketball. His passion for basketball, his work ethic, and competitiveness helped him become a five-time champion. When you sincerely love your craft, and put more into it, you will always rise against the odds to achieve success.

Conclusion

Although Bryant was an exceptional talent, his success was a product of an intense, obsessive work ethic. Bryant's desire to be the best was evident in almost every aspect of his life.

Chapter 16:
10 Habits of Jack Ma

It takes a special person to amass a total net worth of more than $20 billion through hard work and keeping a sense of perspective. Alibaba, one of world's largest e-commerce online platforms, Ceo and founder, Jack Ma is one of the world's wealthiest people, but his success hasn't clouded his strategic direction. Jack Ma's success habits will truly inspire you whether you are an aspiring billionaire or you're a small-business entrepreneur.

To grow his e-commerce business, Jack overcame all difficulties. He had a rough upbringing in communist China. He also failed the college admissions exams twice and was turned down by more than a dozen businesses. He had previously created two failed Internet businesses. However, the third time, Alibaba took off swiftly.

Here are 10 things you can grasps from Jack Ma success journey:

1. **Giving Up is Failing**

Jack Ma is one person who understands the meaning of failure, as it started in his early days. He founded two companies which terribly failed before the success of Alibaba. For Ma, giving up is failure.

Give your grind your best shot even when the struggle is real. Failing shouldn't make you give up, instead make sure you see the goal through to the end. Hardship is your learning lesson, and understanding its lessons is the key to fortune.

2. Let Your Initiative Impact on Society Positively

Ma created his vision focusing on its impactful influence on consumers. He also notes that consumer's happiness should be the end goal rather than the profits.

Let your entrepreneurial path be the reason why people's lives are improving. This results will be in long-term-positive business relationships.

3. What's Matters Is Where You Finish

Your humble beginnings shouldn't prevent you from taking chances. Your spirit, toughness, grit, and fortitude will tell whether or not you'll succeed.

What matters is whether you are putting much effort as needed and this will tell how determined you are to succeed. Dig in your heels, like Jack Ma, and give every opportunity your all.

4. Act Swiftly

According to Jack Ma, you must be extremely quick in seizing opportunities. To win in the end, you must first be off the starting line. You must also be quick to recover from and learn from mistakes. Grab an opportunity that is in your line of sight as soon as you see it and work with it before anyone else does. This will elevate you above your competitors, who are merely competent.

5. Persistence

Ma believes that leaders must be tenacious and with a clear vision. Understanding what you want and having the drive to pursue it will not only put you on the path to success, but will also inspire those around you to work hard to achieve their goals. Ma's business concept is around taking pleasure in one's job and refusing to accept no for an answer.

6. Foresightedness

A good leader, according to Jack Ma, should have foresight. As a leader, it's good that you're always one step ahead of the competition by anticipating how decisions will be implemented before others. Invest your time in developing creative strategies while intensifying a trait where you always follow a knowledge-based intuition.

7. Take a risk

Ma founded Alibaba Group, a very successful conglomerate of internet enterprises, in the face of skepticism from potential investors. The perfect time to take risks, is when you are pursuing your chosen goal path-when criticism is at its core.

8. Be Prepared to Fail

Jack Ma is no stranger to failure. He applied to college three times before being accepted. He created two unsuccessful companies before success of Alibaba. Even KFC didn't think he was a good fit.

When you give up on your first try, you are turning your life around. As probably you'll move on to something else while ending your dreams.

9. Take Chances When You're Still Young

Ma believes that if you are not wealthy by the age of 35, you have squandered your youth. Take use of your youth's vitality and imagination by succumbing to your goal and pursuing it.

Accept and learn from every opportunity that comes your way while you're still young. Grab every opportunity and make best of it by giving it your all. Your ability to pick up any job will help you develop tenancy.

10. Live life

Ma has a reputation for not taking things too seriously. Despite his hectic schedule, he always finds time to relax and enjoy life. If you work your whole life, you will undoubtedly come to regret it.

Conclusion

Jack Ma is one of most inspiring person in the world. His struggle way up and desire for wealth continues to inspire. Through his experience, Jack Ma demonstrates how as an entrepreneur, you can bring ambition to life.

Chapter 17: How To Stop Feeling Overwhelmed

There might come a million instances in your life when you will feel overwhelmed. Whether it's college, work, social obligations, family, or life in general, life can get anxious, stressed, and overwhelmed at certain times. It's important to recognize these feelings and give yourself grace when you have these feelings. Try to dive deeper into your emotions and understand what's causing them, don't brush them off or push through whatever's causing you to feel anxious. Your mental health matters more than anything, and if you're feeling the squeeze, know that you can always take a step back.

When things start to feel a little too much for you, take a deep breath and step away. If you feel anxious or overwhelmed, start doing some breathing exercises to alleviate those feelings. If the thing that's causing you anxiety is right in front of you, take a step away from it and create some separation between you that's overwhelming you. Deep breathing exercises will promote relaxation and would lower your stress response immediately. Understand that we all go through these phases, and it's completely okay and normal to feel like this. Cut yourself some slack and be kind towards yourself. If you're unable to do that chore or have to ask for some extension in your deadline, then do that. Your mental health should be your top priority.

While most of the time, we might want to get isolated or want everyone to leave us alone in our times of stress and anxiety, it's better to reach out to a loved one and ask for their support and help. You can also virtually chat to an online psychologist and rant to them to feel better. Or you can pick up the phone and call your friends or family and ask for their comfort and consolation.

You can also find a hobby that you find relaxation in. It can either be swimming, driving, baking, reading, or any of the stuff that calms your mind and you enjoy doing it. Writing down your reasons for anxiousness and being overwhelmed can also be a great way to alleviate those feelings. It helps you express yourself freely and provides a sense of relief once all of those thoughts are out of your head. Always remember that whatever you're feeling is temporary. With the right coping mechanisms and support, you can always take care of yourself when things start to go south. Protect your time and space and create healthy boundaries for yourself.

Chapter 18:

10 Habits of Warren Buffett

Who does not know Warren Buffett? The multi-billionaire whose vast empire has built him a reputation nobody can dispute. Every businessperson aspires to be him someday.

These are the ten habits of Warren Buffett:

1. <u>He Is Progressive</u>

The man the world knows as wealthy was not born rich. At the age of twenty years, he had a paltry net worth of $20,000. Over the next seventy years, he has grown steadily to have a net worth of $103.8 billion. This is an indication of his progress over the years.

He is a testament to the saying hard work pays. Progress in his business empires is evident in the tax returns he pays to his country.

2. <u>He Is Patriotic</u>

Warren Buffet is a patriotic American citizen who duly remits taxes and abides by the law. In October 2016 during America's presidential elections, Mr. Buffett rose to the challenge of his rivals that he does not pay taxes. He came out clean and said that he has copies of all seventy-two of his returns and that he has paid federal income tax every year since 1944.

He also has no criminal record and no conviction of any crime whatsoever. By all measures and standards, he is a patriotic citizen.

3. <u>He is Business-Oriented</u>

A majority if not all the wealth Mr. Buffett has amassed is attributed to his businesses and not a salary. You cannot grow into the man he is today if you solely depend on your paycheck. You must be open-minded to venture into different businesses.

Warren Buffett runs his parent company, Berkshire Hathaway, which owns other companies like Duracell and Dairy Queen restaurant chain.

4. <u>He is a Humble Person.</u>

Mr. Warren Buffett is not a proud man despite being among the wealthiest people on the planet. If somebody else were in his position, he/she could have misused it. They could probably trample on the needy and the poor. This has never been Mr. Warren's character.

The soft-spoken man is humble in word and deed even when he is provoked into an argument as he was in 2016 regarding tax evasion claims by his rivals.

5. <u>He Is Courageous</u>

His courage in business is when he went against the norms of buying shares when no one was buying. He was buying when everybody else was selling. This is a bold move because there is uncertainty on the performance of the company issuing shares.

His courage also helped him overcome the fear of public speaking while he was young. Without it, he could not be the man he is today.

6. <u>He Gives Free Advice</u>

The most memorable advice that Mr. Buffett gave was to be fearful when others are greedy. He advises against following a popular opinion blindly. In investment, it pays to take a step back when other investors are buying shares greedily.

Mr. Buffett advises different groups of people whenever he gets the opportunity. He is not shy to share his wisdom and experience with the upcoming generation.

7. <u>He is a Generous Philanthropist.</u>

What do we call a man who pledged to give 99% of his wealth to philanthropy during his lifetime or at death? He is generous and very charitable. He has been supporting the needy and vulnerable in society.

So generous is Mr. Buffett that he made history in 2006 by donating $37 billion to the Bill and Melinda Gates Foundation – the largest-ever individual charity donation.

8. <u>He is Modest</u>

The multi-billionaire still lives in the house he bought in the 1950s and is driving a modest car. He does not show off his wealth, neither does he live the lifestyle his fellow billionaires do. He lives comfortably and is quoted saying he does not need money, the society does more.

His modesty is enviable and rare. It makes him stand out from the rest in his pool.

9. <u>He is Selfless</u>

Usually, the rich would want to continue amassing more wealth for themselves as is the practice globally. Mr. Warren is selfless to put the needs of others ahead of their own. This habit is evident in his many generous charitable donations.

10. <u>He Has Enough Sleep</u>

According to the Insider, Mr. Warren Buffett sleeps eight hours a night. He values his time to rest and adheres to it so that he can wake up feeling fresh to face the new day. He wakes up at 6:45 am before reading newspapers.

In conclusion, these ten habits of Warren Buffett form his lifestyle.

Chapter 19:
10 Habits of Cristiano Ronaldo

Cristiano Ronaldo dos Santos Aveiro, famously known as Cristiano Ronaldo, was born on 5th February 1985 in Funchal, Madeira, Portugal. He is the last born in a family of four children. His father, José Dinis Aveiro, named the football legend after his favorite actor – Ronald Reagan.

Here are ten habits of Cristiano Ronaldo:

1. **He pursues his dreams.**

Nothing stands in the way of Ronaldo and his dreams. In an interview with British reporters, his godfather – Fernao Sousa – recalls how young Ronaldo loved soccer. He could escape out of his bedroom window with a ball when he ought to be doing his homework. He could even skip meals to go play soccer.

Cristiano Ronaldo has played for great clubs like Manchester United, Real Madrid, Juventus and his national team – Portugal.

2. **He knows how to package himself.**

Cristiano Ronaldo is one of the highly paid professional soccer players globally. Manchester United paid £12.24 million for young Ronaldo and he joined the club on 12th August 2003. It was a lot of money for a teenager but his expertise in soccer was unmatched.

On 11th June 2009, he left Manchester United for Real Madrid after the latter paid $131 million! His transfer from the London club was imminent but nobody expected such a high price could be paid for his services.

3. He is hardworking.

Ronaldo trains hard to play the best football game ever. His performance with Portugal against Manchester United amazed everybody and the club signed the young player after some of their players asked their manager to do so.

He told reporters that he was aware of the pressure to perform he would have at Real Madrid but he was up to the task. He confessed that he was ready for new challenges for him to become the best footballer.

4. He knows how to handle victory.

Cristiano Ronaldo has not let victory cloud his judgement. He has maintained his rationality despite being the world's most celebrated soccer player. He knows the responsibility on his shoulders of being a role model to many people globally.

He has bagged many awards in his football career including best Fifa Men's player (twice), ballon d'or (five times), UEFA best player in Europe (thrice), European champion, Champions league winner (five times) and many more. Cristiano Ronaldo has guarded himself from pride despite global recognition and all the accolades he has won.

5. He knows how to keep things private.

Ronaldo is a global football icon and his life is constantly under constant watch. It is almost impossible for him to live a private life. He is aware of this and has tried a lot to keep his personal life under wraps.

He has kept the status of his relationship to Georgina Rodriguez private with Italian media speculating that they had wed in Morocco. The couple has not come out to clear the air. The only information in the public is that they have a daughter together.

6. <u>He loves parenting.</u>

The football superstar loves parenting. He is not an absentee father. His relationship with his children is very good. He often trains his son – Cristiano junior – how to play soccer like him. A video of Ronaldo senior training with Ronaldo junior garnered 4 million views in 30 minutes on Instagram.

It is evident that the five times ballon d'or winner is doing a good job as a parent and coach because his son has scored 58 goals in only 28 games for the under-9s in Juventus.

7. <u>He is responsible.</u>

Cristiano Ronaldo is a responsible person. When he was still in Juventus, Massimiliano Allegri, tasked Ronaldo with the responsibility of inspiring the younger players in the team.

He confessed that Ronaldo is a great player and smart guy. He has never been the team captain at Juventus nor at Manchester United but he is a responsible team player and has been coordinating the team within and without the pitch.

8. <u>He values family.</u>

Ronaldo has demonstrated the importance of family. He had a close relationship with his father until the former succumbed to kidney related problems. He wanted his father to go to rehab to cure his alcoholism addiction but he declined his son's offer.

The football star has also taken care of his family by buying them a property worth £ 7 million in Portugal. He prioritizes the well-being of his family over anything in his life.

9. <u>He is generous.</u>

Cristiano is a generous man. He once sold a golden boot award in an auction that raised more than a million Euros. The proceeds were channeled towards building schools in Gaza. He similarly auctioned his award for best player of the year in 2017 and the funds were donated to the Make-A-Wish foundation.

He recently took a pay cut from March to June 2021 that cost him 3.8 million euros. He has also donated almost one million euros to hospitals in Portugal aid in the fight against the coronavirus pandemic.

10. <u>He is patriotic.</u>

Ronaldo is a patriotic citizen to his motherland, Portugal. He has lead the national soccer team to the world cup several times and also in European tournaments as the team captain. It is conspicuous that he has never been the team captain for any of the football clubs he has played for.

He accepted to pay a £ 16.6 million fine over tax evasion charges. He acted how a patriotic citizen would do instead of battling it in court to maneuver the charges against him.

In conclusion, these are the ten habits of the world's soccer G.O.A.T (greatest of all time).

Chapter 20:
<u>Motivation With Good Feelings</u>

Ever wonder what goes on in your mind when you feel depressed isn't always the reaction to the things that happen to you? What you go through when you feel down is the chemistry of your brain that you yourself allow being created in the first place.

You don't feel weak just because your heart feels so heavy. You feel weak because you have filled your heart with all these feelings that don't let you do something useful.

Feelings are not your enemy till you choose the wrong ones. In fact, Feelings and emotions can be the strongest weapon to have in your arsenal.

People say, "You are a man, so act like one. Men don't cry, they act strong and brave"

You must make yourself strong enough to overcome any feelings of failure or fear. Any thought that makes you go aloof and dims that light of creativity and confidence. It's OK to feel sad and cry for some time, but it's not OK to feel weak for even a second.

Your consciousness dictates your feelings. Your senses help you to process a moment and in turn help you translate them into feelings that go both ways. This process has been going on from the day you were born and will continue till your last day.

You enter your consciousness as soon as you open your eyes to greet the day. It is at this moment when your creativity is at its peak. What you need now is just a set of useful thoughts and emotions that steer your whole day into a worthwhile one.

Don't spend your day regretting and repressing things you did or someone else did to you. You don't need these feelings right now. Because you successfully passed those tests of life and are alive still to be grateful for what you have right now.

There are a billion things in life to be thankful for and a billion more to be sad for. But you cannot live a happy fulfilling life if you focus on the later ones.

Life is too short to be sad and to be weak. When you start your day, don't worry about what needs to be done. But think about who you need to be to get those things done.
Don't let actions and outcomes drive you. Be the sailor of yourself to decide what outcomes you want.

Believe me, the feeling of gratitude is the biggest motivator. Self gratitude should be the level of appraisal to expect. Nothing should matter after your own opinions about yourself.

If you let other people's opinions affect your feelings, you are the weakest person out there. And failure is your destination.

Visualization of a better life can help you feel and hope better. It would help you to grow stronger and faster but remember; The day you lose control of your emotions, feelings, and your temper, your imagination will only lead you to a downward spiral.

Chapter 21:
10 Habits of Steve Jobs

Steven Paul Jobs was an American innovator, designer, and undoubtedly successful businessman. He is a narrative of entrepreneurial creation myth: he transformed imagination into technology and entrepreneur skills. He helped usher in an era of personal and tablet computing, smartphones, animated films, music, digital publishing, and retail outlets.

Steve founder Apple in his parents' garage in 1976 was ousted in 1985, but later returned to the company to save it when it was a purge of bankruptcy; by the time of his death in 2011, he transformed it into the world's most valuable company. Even if Steve is no longer here, his legacy will live on.

Here are 10 Steve Jobs habits that are worth your attention.

1. You Can Anticipate the Future

Steve Jobs is still a living example of someone who can predict future trends. His efforts have benefited Apple, as evidenced by the company's dominance in digital sales. The iPhone has transformed the phone market by introducing a very sophisticated touch-screen phone. One way to incorporate this into your life is by imagining yourself in years to come because having a vision will help you anticipate, prepare for hurdles and overcome them.

2. Don't Let Circumstances Limit Your Life.

Master a habit of seeing the positive in every situation and creating a channel to reap its benefits. As an adoptive child, Steve may easily have despised his upbringing or perhaps indulged in undesirable activities as a teenager. Instead, Steve focused on the good; he decided to devote his efforts to technology and computing, and you know how wonderfully that turned out.

3. Find the Ideal Partner

Apple was co-founded by Steve and his partner Steve Wozniak, who greatly complemented Job's skill set. Similarly, to be successful, you must choose the ideal companion in your life. The people you surround yourself with have the power to make or break your life.

4. Don't Sell Crap

While many would argue that Apple only sells high-quality products, you can agree that the quality is the reason why they are still at the top. It is simply through the provision of high-quality products that they have devoted clients who are constantly eager to purchase.

5. Obstacles Are Masked Opportunities

Once you learn to see obstacles as hidden opportunities, you'll always find a way to get away out. During the development of the first Apple computer, Jobs and Wozniak ran out of money. Instead of surrendering, Jobs sold his van, while Wozniak sold his graphing calculator. There is always a way when there is a will.

6. Take That Risk

Steve was willing to give up his company's products for the sake of advancement. Many CEOs would have been hesitant to develop an iPhone, knowing that it would almost certainly lead to the collapse of the iPod-but Jobs did it nonetheless. To progress, you must risk it. However, to make an informed decision, assess the risk's best and worst-case scenarios.

7. To Sell Your Idea, First Assess Whether it's Fit.

Compared to other companies, one thing unique about Steve and Apple is that Apple surprises the world with a new product that you could never have imagined. That is an example of empathy. That is seeing the world as it should be rather than as it is.

8. Redefine the Game

Rather than focusing on beating your competitors, redefine your game. Apple Inc. went from being on the verge of bankruptcy to releasing the iPhone ten years later because Steve played a computer game that other competitors didn't. While other smartphones featured physical keyboards, Apple developed touch-screen smartphones that most users preferred.

9. Explore the World and Try New Things

As an entrepreneur, traveling opens new windows and avenues. You must understand people from different places to instigate a consumerist understanding. After traveling to Ashram, India, Steve noted how it opened his mind to new market ideas in an interview.

10. Learning as a Child

According to Steve Jobs, learning is a continuous habit and an essential skill of success. Each time you learn a new thing, it reshapes your brain and enhances your focus. Consider how children approach learning in different ways. To them, it's merely a component of the exploration they utilize to confront the world around them.

Conclusion

Just like Steve Jobs, it all comes down to the initial step. If you have an idea, put it into action. It will die out if you do not start. Believe in your vision and get started.

Chapter 22:
How To Set Smart Goals

Setting your goals can be a tough choice. It's all about putting your priorities in such a way that you know what comes first for you. It's imperative to be goal-oriented to set positive goals for your present and future. You should be aware of your criteria for setting your goals. Make sure your plan is attainable in a proper time frame to get a good set of goals to be achieved in your time. You would need hard work and a good mindset for setting goals. Few components can help a person reach their destination. Control what you choose because it will eternally impact your life.

To set a goal to your priority, you need to know what exactly you want. In other words, be specific. Be specific in what matters to you and your goal. Make sure that you know your fair share of details about your idea, and then start working on it once you have set your mind to it. Get a clear vision of what your goal is. Get a clear idea of your objective. It is essential to give a specification to your plan to set it according to your needs.

Make sure you measure your goals. As in, calculate the profit or loss. Measure the risks you are taking and the benefits you can gain from them. In simple words, you need to quantify your goals to know what order to set them into. It makes you visualize the amount of time it will take or the energy to reach the finish line. That way, you can calculate your goals and their details. You need to set your mind on the positive technical growth of your goal. That is an essential step to take to put yourself to the next goal as soon as possible.

If you get your hopes high from the start, it may be possible that you will meet with disappointment along the way. So, it would be best if you made sure that your goals are realistic and achievable. Make sure your goal is within reach. That is the reality check you need to force in your mind that is your goal even attainable? Just make sure it is, and everything will go as planned. It doesn't mean to set small goals. There is a difference between big goals and unrealistic goals. Make sure to limit your romantic goals, or else you will never be satisfied with your achievement.

Be very serious when setting your goals, especially if they are long-term goals. They can impact your life in one way or another. It depends on you how you take it. Make sure your goals are relevant. So, that you can gain real benefit from your goals. Have your fair share of profits from your hard work and make it count. Always remember why the goal matters to you. Once you get the fundamental idea of why you need this goal to be achieved, you can look onto a bigger picture in the frame. If it doesn't feel relevant, then there is no reason for you to continue working for. Leave it as it is if it doesn't give you what you applied for because it will only drain your energy and won't give you a satisfactory outcome.

Time is an essential thing to keep in focus when working toward your goals. You don't want to keep working on one thing for too long or too short. So, keep a deadline. Keep a limit on when to work on your goal. If it's worth it, give it your good timer, but if not, then don't even waste a second on it. They are just some factors to set your goals for a better future. These visionary goals will help you get through most of the achievements you want to get done with.

Chapter 23:

10 Habits of Drake

Aubrey Drake Graham, famously known as Drake, was born on 26th October 1986 in Toronto, Canada. Drake was born a musician – a trait from his family roots.

Here are ten habits of Drake:

1. <u>He identifies himself with his African heritage.</u>

Although Drake was born outside Africa, he is proud of the African culture where his father hails from. In an interview, he once said that he considers himself more of a Black man than White.

He is not shy of his African descent. When sharing about his childhood, he recalls that he was raised by his mother in a Jewish setting and he felt out of place in a high school of dominant white people.

2. <u>He loves acting.</u>

Drake rose to fame in a teen drama series *Degrassi: The Next Generation* where he played the role of Jimmy Brooks. So great was his passion for acting that he dropped out of school to pursue acting as a career.

He starred in *Degrassi* from 2001 to 2009. This was something Drake as a teen had not envisaged in his life. He landed the acting role after his classmate's father had asked his son to have anyone who made him laugh at school audition for him.

3. <u>He is hardworking.</u>

The young Graham managed to build a name for himself just a year after appearing in *Degrassi*. In 2002, he bagged a young artist award. This was the beginning of his star shining brighter.

He has worked hard in his music career and won a Grammy award for the best rap album, *Take care* in 2013. His hard work has put him in a position to mingle with giants in the music industry both in America and Canada.

4. He has thick skin.

Drake has developed a thick skin against scandals in his music career. He once had a bitter rivalry with Chris Brown as they were competing for Rihanna's love. This erupted into violence and both were sued for damages by those who were hurt in the incident.
Nothing has derailed his journey in music. He was once sued by his former girlfriend over her input in co-writing *Marvin's Room*. She was seeking credit for it but Drake managed to settle the matter out of court.

5. He is aggressive.

Drake does not take insults lying down. He responds with fire for fire. He has found himself in feuds with Tyga and Meek Mill. In 2015, Meek alleged that Drake was using a ghostwriter for a song they were collaborating.
Drake recorded and released two diss tracks aimed at Meek Mill within a single week. In the following year, he was also in another war of words with Joe Budden.

6. He has a strong determination.

Drake is a strong-willed person and nothing obscures his way to success. They may only delay him but not prevent him from attaining his goals. This led him to release his famous song *Started from the bottom* in 2013 inspired by his struggle for success.
In an interview with MTV News, Drake is quoted saying that he wanted the world to know through that song that he works hard to be successful. It is not a coincidence.

7. He speaks his mind.

Only a day after his hit single *Hotline Bling* won a Grammy award for the best rap song in 2017, he did not mince his words to the Grammys for pushing him into the rap category. He publicly declined the award.

It is enviable how he speaks his mind without second thoughts. His outspoken nature has earned him fans and foes alike but still he soldiers on.

8. <u>He does not hold grudges.</u>

Drake is a man who does not keep a record of wrongs. He was on bad terms with Chris Brown when they were both competing for Rihanna's attention. It is unthinkable that they would later reunite once more.

He reconciled with Chris Brown and they released a hit song, *No Guidance* in 2019. Drake referred to Chris Brown as the most talented human being on the planet. Drake also championed Meek Mill's release from prison and celebrated Mill's release through social media.

9. <u>He is a great songwriter.</u>

Drake knows how to either subtly or directly throw jabs to his target. His songs are always pregnant with a message for his fans.

He has answered his critics on allegations that he uses a ghostwriter for his lyrics through diss tracks. The latest is *Duppy Freestyle* aimed at rapper Pusha T in 2018.

10. <u>He values family.</u>

Drake has faced allegations from rapper Pusha T that he is a deadbeat father and he is hiding a child. The following month, Drake confirmed Pusha T's claim. He defended himself that he delayed announcing his son's birth because the paternity test was inconclusive.

However, after it was clear that Adonis was his son, Drake could not hold his joy of being a father. He gushed over the toddler and posted pictures of his nuclear family on Instagram.

In conclusion, these are the ten common habits of Drake both in his public and private life.

Chapter 24:
Avoid The Dreaded Burnout

Do you often lack the energy to get on with any new task and feel sluggish throughout most of your day? Do you feel the burden of work that keeps getting pilled up each day?

I know we all try our best to manage everything on our hands and try to bring out the best in us. But while doing so, we engage in too many things and ultimately they take their toll.

It is becoming easier and easier every day where people have more work than ever on their hands. And their sole motive throughout life becomes, to find more and better ways of earning a better living. To find more things to be good and successful at.

We all have things on our hands to complete but let me tell you one thing. You won't be able to continue much longer if you keep with this burnout and exhaustion.

Our body is an engine and it needs a way of cooling down and tuning. So what's the first step you need to reduce burnout? You need to get the right amount of sleep.

There is this myth that you sleep one-third of your life so you don't need an 8-hour sleep. You can easily do the same with four hours and use the other four for more work. Trust me, this is not a myth, it is a misconception about proven research. Your body organs deserve at least half the time of what they spend serving us.

We can refresh and better our focus and cognitive skills once we have a good night's sleep full of dreams.

Another thing that most of us avoid doing is to say No to anyone anytime. The thing is that we don't have any obligation to anyone unless we are bound by a contract of blood or law to do or say anything that anyone tells us to do. The more we feel obligated to anyone, the more we try to do to impress that person or entity with our efforts and conduct.

This attitude isn't healthy for any relation. Excess of anything has never brought any good to anyone. So don't give up everything on just one thing. Instead, try to devise a balance between things. Over-commitment is never a good idea.

The third and final thing I want you to do is to give up on certain things at certain times. You don't need to carry your phone or laptop with you all day. This only creates a distraction even when you don't need to be in that environment.

You don't need to train your subconscious to be always alert on your emails and notifications or any incoming calls all day long. But sometimes you just need to give up on these things and zone out of your repetitive daily life.

Doing your best doesn't always mean giving yourself all out. Sometimes the best productive thing you can do is to relax. And that, my friends, can help you climb every mountain without ever getting tired of trying t do the same trail.

Chapter 25:
9 Habits of Highly Successful People

Success comes to people who deserve it. I bet you have heard this statement quite a few times, right? So, what does it mean exactly? Does it mean that you are either born worthy or unworthy of success? Absolutely not. Everyone is born worthy, but the one thing that makes some people successful is their winning habits and their commitment to these habits.

Today, we will learn how to master ten simple habits and behaviors that will help you become successful.

1. Be an Avid Learner

If you didn't know, almost all of the most successful people in the world are avid learners. So, do not shy away from opportunities when it comes to learning. Wake up each day and look forward to learning new things, and in no time, I bet you will experience how enriching it really is. Also, learning new things has the effect of revitalizing a person. So, if you want to have more knowledge to kickstart your journey in the right direction, here are some things that you can do - make sure to read, even if it is just a page or two, daily. It could be anything that interests you. I personally love reading self-help books. If you are not that much of a reader, you can even listen to a podcast, watch an informative video, or sign up for a course. Choose what piques your interest, and just dive into it!

2. Failure is the Pillar of Success

Most people are afraid to delve into something new, start a new chapter of their lives, and chase after their dreams – all because they are scared to fail. If you are one of those people who are scared to fail, well, don't be! Because what failure actually does is prepares you to achieve your dream. It just makes sure that you are able to handle the success when you finally have it. So when you accept that failure is an inevitable part of your journey, you will be able to plan the right course of action to tackle it instead of just being too scared to move forward. Successful people are never scared of failure; They just turn it around by seeing it as an opportunity to learn.

3. Get Up Early

I bet you have heard this a couple of thousand times already! But whoever told you so was not lying. Almost all successful individuals are early risers! They say that starting the morning right ensures a fruitful day ahead. It is true! Think about it, on the day you get up early, you feel a boost of productivity as compared to when you wake up late and have to struggle against the clock. You will have plenty of time and a good mood to go through the rest of the day which will give you better outcomes. All you have to do is set up a bedtime reminder. This is going to make sure that you enough rest to get up in the morning instead of snoozing your alarm on repeat! Not a morning person? Don't worry. I have got you covered! Start slow and set the alarm 15 minutes before when you usually wake up. It doesn't sound like much, eh? But trust me, you will be motivated to wake up earlier when you see how much difference 15 minutes can make to your day.

4. Have Your Own Morning Ritual

Morning rituals are the most common habit among achievers. It will pump you up to go through the day with a bang! You just have to make a routine for yourself and make sure to follow it every day. You can take inspiration from the morning routines of people you look up to but remember it has to benefit you. So you might be wondering, *What do I include in the ritual?* I would suggest you make your bed first thing in the morning. This might not sound as great a deal, but hey, it is a tested and approved method to boost your productivity. It is even implemented in the military. Doing this will motivate you as you get a sense of achievement as you have completed a task as soon as you woke up. After that, it could be anything that will encourage you, such as a walk, a workout session, reading, journaling, or meditating.

5. Stop Procrastinating

From delaying one task to not keeping up with your deadlines, procrastination becomes a deadly habit. It becomes almost unstoppable! Did you know, most people fail to achieve their dreams even if they have the potential just because of procrastination? Well, they do. And you might not want to become one of them. They say, "Old habits die hard," true, but they do die if you want them to. Procrastination has to be the hardest thing we have to deal with, even though we hey created it in the first place. Trust me, I speak from experience!

So what do you do to stop this? Break your task into small bite-sized pieces. Sometimes, it is just the heaviness of the task that keeps us from doing it. Take breaks in between to keep yourself motivated.

Another thing that you can do is the "minute rule." Divide your tasks by how much time they take. The tasks that take less than 5 minutes, you do it right then. Then you can bigger tasks into small time frames and complete them. Make sure you do not get too lost in the breaks, though!

6. Set Goals

I cannot even begin to tell you how effective goal setting is. A goal gives you the right direction and motivation. It also gives you a sense of urgency to do a task that is going to just take your productivity level from 0 to 10 in no time!

So how do you set goals? Simple. Think about the goals you want to achieve and write them down. But make sure that you set realistic goals. If you find it difficult, don't worry. Start small and slow. Start by making a to-do list for the day. You will find out soo that the satisfaction in ticking those off your list is unbelievable. It will also drive you to tick more of them off!

7. Make Your Health a Priority

Health is Wealth. Yes, it is a fact! When you give your body the right things and make it a priority, it gives you back by keeping you and your mind healthy. I bet you've heard the saying "You are what you eat," and by "eat," it does not simply mean to chew and swallow! It also means that you need to feed your body, soul, and mind with things you want them to be like. Read, listen, learn, and eat healthy. You could set a goal to eat clean for the week. Or workout at least for 10 minutes. And see for yourself how it gives you the energy to smash those goals you've been holding off! Also, great news – you can have cheat days once a week!

8. Plan Your Day the Night Before

"When you fail to plan, you plan to fail." People who succeed in life are not by mere coincidence or luck. It is the result of detailed, focused planning. So, you need to start planning your way to success too. Before you sleep tonight, ask yourself, *What is the most important thing that I have to do tomorrow?* Plan what assignments, meetings, or classes you have to complete. Planning ahead will not only make you organized and ready, it also highly increases your chances to succeed. So, don't forget to plan your day tonight!

9. Master the Habit Loop

Behavioral expert, BJ Fogg, explains that habits are formed around three elements: Cue, Routine, and Reward. Cue is the initial desire that motivates your behavior. Routine is the action you take. And the reward is the pleasure you gain after completion. So why am I telling you all of this? Because this habit loop is how we are wired. It is what motivates us. We seek pleasure and avoid pain. And you can use this loop to your advantage! Let's say you want to finish an assignment. Think of the reason why you want to. Maybe you don't want to fall behind someone or want to impress someone. It could be anything! Now time for you to set your rewards. It could be eating a slice of cheesecake or watching an episode of your favorite series after you've finished. Rewards motivate you when you slack off. Play around until you find a combination that works best for you. You will also need a cue; it could be anything like a notification on your phone, an email, or simply your desire. You can set a cue yourself by creating a reminder.

Habits are what make a man. I hope you follow these habits and start your journey the right way to becoming successful in life.

Chapter 26:

10 Habits of Unsuccessful People

Highly successful people (in any of the many ways that "success" can be defined) seem to recognize a few basic principles. The most important of these is that your energy, not your time, is restricted each day and must be carefully controlled.

Here are 10 of the most popular self-imposed blocks that have a troll on your success. If you come across one, use it as a cue to reevaluate, reflect, and change direction.

1. Worry of the Most Unlikely Outcome.

Despite its label as a "maladaptive trait," worrying has an evolutionary connection to intelligence. This is why, according to Jeremy Coplan, lead author of a study published of Frontiers in Evolutionary Neuroscience, effective people are naturally nervous.

Whatever the case may be, to work correctly, you must be able to distinguish between which fears are worth reacting to and which are your brain's attempt to "prepare" you for survival by conjuring up the most severe possible risk. This is an antiquated, animalistic mechanism that is useless in everyday life. Highly effective people should not spend their time worrying about the things that are least likely to happen.

2. Just Talking the Talk

"I'm preparing to do this and that." What's better than announcing on social media that you're starting a business? Putting it into action.

Entrepreneur Derek Sivers argued in his [2010 TED talk](#), "Keep Your Goals to Yourself," that disclosing your intentions can be detrimental rather than inspiring. People will sometimes applaud you just for stating your purpose, he said, and this applause, ironically, may drain your motivation to carry out the plans you've just outlined.

"Psychotherapists have discovered that telling others your goal and having them embrace it is known as a 'social reality,'" Sivers explained in his talk. "The mind is deceived into believing it has already been accomplished. Then, after you've had your satisfaction, you're less likely to put in the necessary effort."

There's nothing wrong with expressing your happiness. However, try to keep your mouth shut before you have good news, not just good intentions.

3. Ruminating and Not Doing Anything About It

Reflecting becomes ruminating as the intention to act dissolves in favor of constantly replaying certain situations or issues through your mind.

Self-awareness is common among highly successful individuals, or at least it should be. This means they devote a significant amount of time to reflecting on their behavior and experiences and determining how they can change. However, they do not waste mental energy pondering what went wrong rather than consciously modifying what needs to be changed to fix the issue.

4. Choosing the Wrong People To Spend Time With

The people you hang out with can either inspire you to be your best self or bring out your worst traits. Spend time with people who can motivate you to make the changes you want to make in your life. Do you want to fail at that goal completely? If it's the case, spend time with people who gloat about their bad habits. People get their energy from each other. Always remember that you are the average of the 5 people that you spend most of your time with.

5. Being Resentful for Taking Time for Themselves

People who have experienced any degree of success understand that it is a multi-faceted operation. You won't be able to work at your best if you're tired, undernourished, or experiencing some other sort of extreme imbalance in your life.

As a result, highly successful individuals are just as dedicated to relaxation and health as work and efficiency. They don't stress themselves up about how much they should have done in a three-day weekend or why they shouldn't take time off when they need it.

6. Constantly Concentrating on the Negative

It's mind-boggling to focus on the negative aspects of life because it'll only make you feel worse. You don't have to believe that life is simple to concentrate on the positive. You should maintain a rational viewpoint without always pointing out the flaws in everything you see.

We've all met someone who is still complaining about something. "Ugh, it rained this morning, and my shoes were soaked through and through." Yes, that's a disappointment. You won't be able to affect the weather, unfortunately. You should put on a new pair of shoes if you want to.

It's fine if you're having a rough day; we're all irritable at times; everybody gets irritable now and then. However, you are living a poor life if you despise anything. That's what there is to it.

7. Justifying Their Place in Life

Taking on exceptional work also elicits questions and, at times, judgments from those who don't believe in your project or are suspicious of its long-term viability. Constantly feeling the need to explain or justify your role in life, on the other hand, is not only exhausting but also unnecessary. Highly effective people understand that you can't get approval from people who don't want it.

8. Allowing Themselves To Be Sucked Into a State of Laziness

We've all had times when we've been compelled to cancel plans. Leaving the house, even for something "fun," can feel like a Herculean task at times.

However, it is fresh and novel experiences that make life so beautiful. You aren't fully involved in your own life when you succumb to laziness, which is unfair to your friends, family, spouse, and those who want to share it with you.

9. Worrying That Isn't Essential and Unregulated Thought Patterns

Worrying is among the most common ways people drain their energy doing. It is the act of anticipating the worst-case scenario and assuming that it is not only probable but most likely.

Worrying does not make you more equipped to deal with life's challenges instead, it makes you more likely to build your fears. You'd be surprised to learn that 99.9% of your worries were baseless and never "came true" if you made a list of everything you've ever worried about in your life.

If you just made a list of everything you didn't care about in life, you'd find that worrying didn't change anything; it just sapped your energy at the moment. The only thing it has done for you is that it made things more complicated, twisted, and less fun. It is not only ineffective, but completely pointless as well. Highly successful people learn to concentrate on something else rather than spend their time worrying about what could go wrong.

10. There Is Just Too Much Optimistic Thought

It's self-evident that no one achieves remarkable success without first confronting destructive thought patterns. What's less evident is that highly successful people don't partake in excessive positive thinking, which can be arbitrary, distorted, and even distracting in excess. Worse, they set themselves up for failure or disappointment by thinking too positively. Instead, highly successful people understand the power of neutral thought, which means they don't try to make life into something.

Conclusion

If you don't want to be an unsuccessful person, you need to make a conscious effort to avoid doing these things. Focus on the habits that would bring you positive change instead, which we will discuss in another segment.

Chapter 27:
Be Motivated by Challenge

You have an easy life and a continuous stream of income, you are lucky! You have everything you and your children need, you are lucky! You have your whole future planned ahead of you and nothing seems to go in the other direction yet, you are lucky!

But how far do you think this can go? What surety can you give yourself that all will go well from the start to the very end?

Life will always have a hurdle, a hardship, a challenge, right there when you feel most satisfied. What will you do then?

Will you give up and look for an escape? Will you seek guidance? Or will you just give up and go down a dark place because you never thought something like this could happen to you?

Life is full of endless possibilities and an endless parade of challenges that make life no walk in the park.

You are different from any other human being in at least one attribute. But your life isn't much different than most people's. You may be less fortunate or you may be the luckiest, but you must not back down when life strikes you.

This world is a cruel place and a harsh terrain. But that doesn't mean you should give up whenever you get hit in the back. That doesn't mean you don't catch what the world throws at you.

Do you know what you should do? Look around and observe for examples. Examples of people who have had the same experiences as you had and what good or bad things did they do? You will find people on both extremes.

You will find people who didn't have the courage or guts to stand up to the challenge and people who didn't have the time to give up but to keep pushing harder and harder, just to get better at what they failed the last time.

The challenges of life can never cross your limits because the limits of a human being are practically infinite. But what feels like a heavy load, is just a shadow of your inner fear dictating you to give up.

But you can't give up, right? Because you already have what you need to overcome this challenge too. You just haven't looked into your backpack of skills yet!

If you are struggling at college, go out there and prove everyone in their wrong. Try to get better grades by putting in more hours little by little.

If people take you as a non-social person, try to talk to at least one new person each day.

If you aren't getting good at a sport, get tutorials and try to replicate the professionals step by step and put in all your effort and time if you truly care for the challenge at hand.

The motivation you need is in the challenge itself. You just need to realize the true gains you want from each stone in your path and you will find treasures under every stone.

Chapter 28:
Five Habits of Permanent Weight Loss

Weight loss is a journey that many people have embarked on. Some of them are doing so out of personal ambition and others out of a doctor's advice. Regardless of their effort, somehow they seem not to be shedding off enough weight. Sometimes, even after losing a substantial amount of weight, they regain it once more and all their effort goes down the drain.

Here are five habits of permanent weight loss:

1. Win Both The Battle and The War

The mind is the arena of the greatest battle. Regardless that weight gain and loss manifests physically, the mind influences greatly on either outcome. When the battle is lost in the mind, the war against weight gain is subsequently lost.

Train your mind in a manner that suits you to be on the winning side. How so? A disciplined mind will win over your body to adhere to a strict routine geared towards weight loss. When you strengthen your mind not to succumb to temptations that will make you lapse in your weight loss journey, you have won half the battle.

As much as you put strategies in place to follow a particular routine, it is bound to fail if you have a weak mindset. No plan you put in place (that of weight loss included) will ever see the light of day when you are mentally unprepared. Similar to how one exercises body muscles, the brain too needs exercise. When your mind can withstand the temptations of eating anything, permanent weight loss is achievable.

2. Seek Professional Help

The best way to solve a problem is to involve experts. Their insight will diagnose the heart of the problem and prescribe a lasting solution. The journey of weight loss gets easier when you follow the advice of medical doctors. You will know what to do not to cause harm to your body.

The ambition of permanent weight loss may get in your way and make you try wild things to achieve your goal. Some people go to the extent of taking herbal concoctions with the belief that it will help them shed some weight. There are instances where these concoctions have caused more harm than the good they intended.

Most people ignore the advice of doctors regarding weight loss. Instead, they prefer some weird prescription of homemade beverages with the hope of permanent weight loss. There is no shortcut to reaching your goal. When you seek professional help regarding how to adjust your lifestyle, you will not lapse back or add extra weight. Permanent weight loss is achievable.

3. Associate With Like-Minded People

It is said that when you want to go fast, go alone but when you want to go far, go with someone. The journey of weight loss is long when you walk alone. Sometimes you may give up on the way and not achieve your goal.

In the company of people with whom you share a common goal – permanent weight loss –, you will encourage each other. In the small circle of friends, you will be able to exchange ideas and strategies for weight loss. This is unachievable when you isolate yourself.

The major challenge that may initially arise is finding the right group of people with whom you share a common goal. In the wrong group, you will be misplaced and permanent weight loss will forever remain a dream. Actualize this dream by excusing yourself from any rudderless group of people.

4. Lifestyle Change

A lifestyle change is a personal decision that one initiates without any external influence whatsoever. It is a conscious decision that one takes while being fully aware of the disruption it may have on his/her life.

Permanent weight loss is possible when one overhauls his/her lifestyle. When you stop taking alcohol or the habit of always driving even over short distances that you could walk, you will start shedding off some weight. Even an innocent habit of sleeping too much during the day will make you add some weight. Avoid it at all costs.

When you do a lifestyle audit and eliminate habits that will work against your goal of weight loss, the destination of permanent weight loss draws nearer. A lifestyle change is a difficult decision but one worth undertaking.

5. Seek Knowledge

Knowledge is power. Seek correct information on weight loss and avoid dwelling on myths, hearsay, and unfounded beliefs. Misinformation and misplacement of facts about weight loss will make it untenable. The fight against weight gain will have a big boost when there are sufficient facts about it.

The goal is not just weight loss but permanent weight loss. How is it achievable if we lack facts about it? Read and consult widely and approach it from a knowledgeable and informed point of view. Do not act blindly on fallacies.

These five habits for permanent weight loss bring significant change when adhered to.

Chapter 29:
The Magic of Journaling

Today we're going to talk about the power of journaling, and why you should start making it as part of your daily habit starting today.

Everyday, every second of our lives, we are bombarded with things coming at our way. From our colleagues, our bosses, to our friends, families, relationships, and most importantly, ourselves. Life gets hectic and crazy sometimes. We have a million things racing through our minds and we don't have the time or place to let it all out so we keep it bottled up inside.

This creates a backlog of emotions, feelings, things, that we leave undealt with. We start to miss the little details along the way, or our mood gets affected because we can't seem to get rid of the negativity festering up inside of us. If we don't have anyone readily available to talk to us, these feelings that have been building inside of us could end up spilling over and affecting our performance at the workplace, at home, whatever it may be.

We are not able to perform these roles at home or at work effectively as a result. This is where the power of journaling comes into play.

Journaling is such an important tool for us to put into paper or into words every single emotion that we are feeling. Every thought that we are thinking. And this works sort of like a cleanse. We are cleansing, decluttering, and unpacking all the things that are jumbled up in our head. By writing these feelings down, we are not only able to keep a clear head, but it also gives us a reference point to come back to if there are any unresolved problems that we feel we need to work on at a later date.

Journaling has worked wonders for me. I've never thought it to be a habit work incorporating into my life because i thought hey, it's another thing for me to do on top of my already hectic day. I don't have time for this. Basically giving 1001 reasons not to do it.

But I came across this life coach that described the wonders of journaling as I am describing to you right now. And I thought. Why not just give it a try.

I did. And it changed my life.

I never realized how powerful journaling could actually be in transforming my state of mind and to always keep me grounded and focused. Everytime I felt that i was distracted, had something I couldn't work through in my mind, I would pick up my ipad and start typing it down in a journal app.

With technology, it has made journaling a much more enjoyable experience for me and one that i can simply do on the fly, anywhere, anytime. I didn't have to fumble around to find my pen and book, i just opened up the app and started typing away every single feeling and thought.

Journaling helped me see the big picture. It helped me become more aware of the things that are working for me and things that aren't. I was able to focus more on the areas that were bringing more joy in my life and to eliminate the situations and activities that were draining me of my energy and spirit.

Journaling can be anything you want it to be. There are no fixed rules as to how you must journal. Just write whatever comes to your mind. You will be surprised by how much you can learn from yourself. Many a times we forget that we are our best teacher. Other people can't learn our lessons for us, only we can.

So next time you feel sluggish, depressed, unhappy, or even ecstatic and over the moon, write down how and why you got to that place. No judgement, no berating yourself, just pouring your heart and soul onto a piece of paper or into a journaling app. I'll be looking forward to hearing of your transformation from the power of journaling.

Chapter 30:
The 5 Second Rule

Today I'm going to share with you a very special rule in life that has worked wonders for me ever since I discovered it. And that is known as the 5 second rule by Mel Robbins.

You see, on a daily basis, I struggle with motivation and getting things done. I struggle with the littlest things like replying an email, to responding to a work request. This struggle has become such a bad habit that before I think about beginning any sort of work, I would first turn on my Netflix account to watch an episode or two of my favourite sitcom, telling myself that I will get right on it after I satisfy this side of me first.

This habit of procrastination soon became so severe that I would actually sit and end up wasting 4-5 hours of time every morning before I would actually even begin on any work-related stuff. Before I knew it, it would be 3pm and I haven't gotten a single thing done. All the while I was staring at the clock, counting the number of hours I have wasted, while simultaneously addicted to procrastinating that I just could not for the life of me get myself off the couch onto my desk to begin any meaningful work.

I realized that something had to change. If I kept this up, I would not only not get anything done, like ever, but i would also begin to loathe myself for being so incredibly unproductive and useless. This process of self-loathing got worse everyday I leaned into the habit of procrastination. It was only until i stumbled onto Mel Robbin's 5 second rule that I started to see a real change in my habits.

The rule is simple, to count backwards from 5 and to just get up and go do that thing. It sounded stupid to me at first, but it worked. Instead of laying around in bed every morning checking my phone before I woke up, I would count backwards from 5 and as soon as it hit 1, i would get up and head straight towards the shower, or I would pack up my things and get out of my house.

I had identified that staying at home was the one factor that made me the most unproductive person on the planet, and that the only way I knew I was going to get real work done, was to get out of the house. I had also identified that showering was a good way to cleanse my mind from the night before. I really enjoyed showering as I always seem to have a clear head afterwards to be able to focus. What works for me, may not necessarily work for you. You have to identify for yourself when are the times you are most productive, and simply replicate it. A good way to find out is by journaling, which I will talk about in a separate video. Journaling is a good way to capture a moment in time and a particular state of mind. Try it for yourself the next time you are incredibly focused, write down how you got to that state, and simply do it again the next time to get there.

The 5 second rule is so simple yet so powerful because it snaps our unhealthy thought patterns. As Mel puts it, our brain is hardwired to protect us. We procrastinate out of fear of doing the things that are hard, so we have to beat our brain to it by disrupting it first. When we decide to move and take action after reaching 1, it is too late for our brains to stop us. And we get the ball rolling.

I was at my most productive on days that I felt my worst. But I overcame it because I didn't let my brain stop me from myself. I wouldn't say that I am struggle free now, but i knew i had a tool that would work most of the time to get me out of procrastination and into doing some serious work that would move my life forward. There are times when I would forget about the 5 second rule and my bad habits would kick in, but I always reminded myself that it was available to me if I chose to use it.

I would urge all of you who are struggling with any form of procrastination or laziness to give the 5 second rule a try. All you need to do is to get started and the rest becomes easy.

www.ingramcontent.com/pod-product-compliance
Lightning Source LLC
LaVergne TN
LVHW010347070526
838199LV00065B/5802